Contents

These Notes are based on the Heinemann paper
edition of *Selected Poems and Letters of John Keats*,
Edited with an Introduction and Commentary by
Robert Gittings, but as Part and line references
are made to the different poems, these Notes may
be used with other editions of Keats's works.

Graham Handley MA PHD

Brodie's Notes on

Selected Poems and Letters of John Keats

Pan Educational London and Sydney

First published 1978 by Pan Books Ltd
Cavaye Place, London SW10 9PG
1 2 3 4 5 6 7 8 9
© Graham Handley 1978
ISBN 0 330 50126 7
Filmset in Great Britain by
Northumberland Press Ltd, Gateshead, Tyne and Wear
Printed and bound by
Richard Clay (The Chaucer Press) Ltd, Bungay, Suffolk

The author and his work

The chronology of Keats's brief life is a straightforward one. He was born in October 1795 in Finsbury, London, the son of Thomas Keats and his wife Frances, whose maiden name was Jennings. In the next few years two boys and a girl were born to his parents, and in 1803 Keats began to attend what was for those times an enlightened school, Clarke's school at Enfield. But in 1804 his father died, and within two months his mother had married again and the children moved to their grandparents' home in Enfield. There was another move in the next year to Edmonton, with Keats continuing at the Enfield school and becoming friendly with the son of the headmaster, Charles Cowden Clarke, with whom he had many stimulating talks and walks. In March 1810 his mother died, and his grief was intense. In the summer of that year he left school and began an apprenticeship with Thomas Hammond, a surgeon in Edmonton, while his brothers became clerks under the auspices of their guardian, Richard Abbey. By 1813 his first attempt in verse ('Imitation of Spenser') indicated the direction his future interests would take; but in the following year he entered Guy's hospital as a student and lived in lodgings close by.

1816 sees the beginning of Keats's literary career proper with a sonnet published in Leigh Hunt's *Examiner*, and the writing of the remarkable 'On First Looking Into Chapman's Homer'. And there were meetings with Leigh Hunt, the painter Haydon, who was to be an early influence on him, and John Hamilton Reynolds. At the same time he qualified at the Apothecaries' Hall. In 1817 he moved to Hampstead and in March his first book of verse, *Poems*, was published; most of the year was given to the writing of *Endymion*, during which time he stayed at Margate and in the Isle of Wight and devoted himself to a detailed study of Shakespeare. He also stayed with his friend Bailey in Oxford and spent some time reading *Paradise Lost*. Keats's letters at this time bear witness to his preoccupation with poetry and to his formulation of his own creed: 'Beauty is Truth'; and the idea of 'Negative Capability'. *Endymion* was published in April 1818, while from June to August he went on a walking tour with Brown in the Lake District and in Scotland. But when he returned to London in August, suffering from a sore throat, he found his brother Tom was seriously ill. He nursed Tom, began to write 'Hyperion' and had to bear the savage reviews of *Endymion* (notably in *Blackwood's* and *The Quarterly Review*).

In the autumn of that year he met Fanny Brawne. He had already written *Isabella*, but in a letter to Woodhouse set forth the idea of the 'camelion [*sic*] Poet' who is subject to all kinds of experience but lacks an identity. The shattering effect of his brother Tom's death in December 1818 was to be felt for a long time afterwards; and in fact Keats was to recur to it throughout his poetry and letter-writing life. In January 1819 Keats visited Chichester with Brown, writing 'The Eve of St Agnes' in that month and following it with the 'Eve of St Mark' in the next; the spring was given over to the Odes and also to 'La Belle Dame Sans Merci', and he decided to abandon 'Hyperion'. His new neighbours in Wentworth Place were the Brawnes, but he stayed in the Isle of Wight again and wrote part of 'Lamia' as well as some of 'The Fall of Hyperion'. Later, in September, he wrote the 'Ode to Autumn' in Winchester, and stated in a letter that his greatest ambition was to write plays. Early in 1819 he became engaged to Fanny Brawne, but by February 1820 he had suffered the haemorrhage which signified the beginning of the end. 'Ode on a Grecian Urn' and 'La Belle Dame Sans Merci' were published in magazines during the year, but the major event was the issuing of *Lamia, Isabella, The Eve of St Agnes and Other Poems* by Taylor and Hessey. During August he was being nursed by Fanny Brawne; but, on doctor's advice, sailed for Italy in September with his friend Joseph Severn. On 23 February 1821 he died, and three days later was buried in the English Cemetery in Rome.

This is the merest outline of a life and a legend of unparalleled richness in the history of literature and scholars and writers return with unflagging interest to its main facets. *The Selected Poems and Letters of Keats* by Robert Gittings contains all of Keats's major works – either in full or in generous extract – and many of the important statements Keats made about poetry and about life in his letters. And the introductions supplied by Gittings, both biographical and critical, are essential reading for the student.

The influences on Keats were many. He looked back to the Elizabethans, being at first so impressed by Spenser that he wrote avowedly Spenserian imitations; and it is interesting to note that the stanza of *The Faerie Queene* is used with great maturity in 'The Eve of St Agnes'; and, with a rather different emphasis, in the last poem he wrote, 'The Cap and Bells'. He also looked back to Shakespeare, and if his blank verse effects are generally more Miltonic than Shakespearian, there is the fragment, 'King Stephen' to show how much Keats absorbed of the greatest of our dramatists. He absorbed, too, that mastery of the sonnet possessed by both Shakespeare and Milton; the narrative art of Chaucer; the vivid and unusual and subtle evocations of Dante; the esoteric derivations of Chatterton. His contemporaries Wordsworth and Coleridge, in the van of the Romantic movement, bequeathed to him both the mystical and the simple. By the time he came to write *Lamia* he had saturated himself in Dryden too. He made the form of the ode his own and gave the rhyming couplet a less end-stopped, freer movement than in, say, Pope or Dryden. And beyond all this is his undying interest in things pagan, going right back to that early attempt at translation of the *Aeneid* and reading adaptations, re-tellings, *The Anatomy of*

Melancholoy, whatever came to hand, fed his remarkable sensibility – we can only marvel at his stamina in the short time at his disposal; so much did he read, so consciously did he live.

Imitating much, whether consciously or unconsciously, Keats was certainly nobody's slave but his own; subjecting himself to the influences of the senses and of the past, he saw vividly and memorably but with his own eyes; we may mark the influences in his work, but also take account of his own unique creativity. He is a visual poet, a writer of the senses and feelings, but his poems and letters bear eloquent witness to the quality of his thought.

The poem-by-poem commentary that follows this introductions is intended as a small supplement to Mr Gittings's own introduction and notes. Reference is made to the influences on Keats wherever possible, and also to the forms he uses; for this reason a short list of terms follows this brief preliminary to the poems, but students using words like 'alliteration', 'simile' or 'assonance' should not treat them as labels, for in themselves such simple definitions are never enough. What matters is what a poet achieves and how he achieves it; and good criticism should attempt to explain this, rather than fall back on a terminology that categories without evaluation. Keats, like all poets, must be read with attention and vision, attributes he himself brought to his writing. These Notes will, it is hoped, involve the student in some of the experiences of that writing, but they can never be a substitute for the reading of the poems and letters themselves.

Lastly, the writer of these Notes would like to acknowledge with gratitude Robert Gittings's generosity in reading, and suggesting alterations for, this commentary.

Further reading

John Keats The Living Year Robert Gittings (Heinemann)
John Keats Robert Gittings (Heinemann)
Keats: The Complete Poems edited by Miriam Allott (Longman)
John Keats: The Making of a Poet Aileen Ward
(Secker & Warburg)

Definitions of terms

Below will be found a list of terms used in the Notes to define certain aspects of the poet's art; these are commonly used in the evaluation of poetry, which, like other arts, has its own vocabulary, but that vocabulary can in no sense be a substitute for the immediate response of the individual reader.

Alliteration This is the repetition of the first sound of several words in a line or passage, as in the opening of Shakespeare's sonnet, 'When to the sessions of sweet silent thought . . .'

Allegory *The Concise Oxford Dictionary* definition of this term is 'Narrative description of a subject under guise of another suggestively similar.' Many of Keats's poems have an allegorical content, for example 'The Ode to a Nightingale' and 'The Fall of Hyperion'.

Analogy The word means proportion, agreement, similarity, and in literary terms this means an argument or description that finds its parallel in another argument or description.

Antithesis This is the contrast of ideas expressed by the parallelism of strongly contrasted words; a direct opposite. The classical example is Pope's line, 'To err is human; to forgive, divine.'
There are, as one might expect, examples of this in 'Lamia'.

Assonance This is stressed vowels agreeing or rhyming, but not the consonants. It is common in a later poet, Wilfred Owen, but in Keats this only occurs within the lines (like 'deep' and 'demesne' in *'On First Looking Into Chapman's Homer'*).

Ballad These always have a narrative element, and Coleridge's *Rime of the Ancient Mariner* is a good example. 'La Belle Dame Sans Merci' is in the ballad form.

Bathos Anti-climax, a descent in terms of poetic level; images, metaphors, descriptions or statements that lower the standard of the writing and/or the quality of the thought. Examples in Keats occur in both 'Isabella' and 'Lamia'.

Blank verse This verse is not in rhyme, and derives from the verse of Shakespeare's plays and of Milton's *Paradise Lost*. Here Milton describes it as 'English Heroic verse, without Rime', and its influence on both versions of 'Hyperion' was considerable. Keats eventually abandoned Miltonic verse because of the inversion of language it required.

Couplet Two lines of verse, usually rhyming and in the same metre, forming a unit in themselves. An end-stopped line has a logical pause at its close (frequently met with in the poetry of Pope, and also Dryden, who was an influence on the writing of 'Lamia'), while a run-on line is exactly what it says, the sense running over to the succeeding line. *Triplets* are three successive lines having the same rhyme; an *alexandrine* is a twelve-syllabled line which rhymes with the preceding couplet, which usually has ten syllables per line; the *iambic pentameter* is a ten-syllabled line with the stress on every second syllable (found particularly in sonnets).

Epithet This is an adjective which expresses the quality or attribute of the thing it describes. Keats uses double-barrelled epithets: (for example 'sapphire-regioned' to describe a star in *'The Eve of St Agnes'*.

Images and imagery The representation of a thing with evocative (usually metaphorical) detail, though this detail need not be visual; it may appeal to the senses, as frequently in Keats, or it may be open to symbolic interpretation.

Internal rhymes This is a device whereby the lines have words within them which rhyme with those at the end of the lines. Keats sometimes uses this effectively.

Invocation This is calling upon God (or man, or some form of being) in prayer, or appealing for assistance or guidance in a direct manner. Frequently the word 'O' begins an invocation; Keats is very fond of using it: for instance in 'Hyperion', while he builds 'The Ode to Psyche' from it as a beginning.

Lyric and Lyrical A lyric is a poem composed to be sung or appropriate for singing, and generally it expresses the feeling of the person voicing it. Certain passages in Keats's verse are lyrical in tone.

Ode This is a lyric which is exalted in form or manner, and is generally elaborately constructed. Choral odes were composed by the Greek poet Pindar, and Collins, Dryden and Gray are among the English poets who have written formal Pindaric odes. Keats experiments with the Ode, finally bringing it to perfection in 'The Ode to a Nightingale' and 'To Autumn'.

Onomatopoeia The use of words that imitate or directly echo the sound of the thing described (e.g. 'buzz', 'hiss', 'chatter').

Pathos This is the quality in verse or speech or music which excites pity or sadness; it must not be confused with BATHOS, which, as we have seen, is anti-climax.

Pun This is the humorous use of a word to suggest its different meanings, or the use of words of the same sound which have different meanings. It is the basis of word-play. Keats uses this occasionally, and has half-puns too ('O Attic shape! Fair attitude').

Quatrains This is simply a four-lined verse (or stanza), often, though not necessarily, with alternate lines rhyming. It is not much used by Keats.

Simile A comparison introduced by 'like' or 'as', as distinct from a *metaphor*, which is a comparison, often sustained, without formal introduction. As Aristotle observed, a command of metaphor is 'the mark of genius, for to make good metaphors implies an eye for resemblances'. Keats has this eye *par excellence*.

Sonnet This is a poem of fourteen lines, normally in iambic pentameter, divided into an octave and a sestet (eight and six lines respectively), and generally concerned with a single thought or feeling; this is virtually in two paragraphs on the same subject, divisions of thought as well as rhyme. Keats is a fine sonneteer, using Elizabethan and other models, ranging over the English and Italian forms, and using a variety of rhyming structures.

Stanzas These are regular subdivisions of a poem. This means that each stanza or verse has a requisite number of lines, the same numbers of feet and stresses in corresponding lines, and with a regular rhyme scheme. Small letters of the alphabet are sometimes used to indicate the rhyme scheme (for example *abab* in a stanza where the first line rhymes with the third, and the second line with the fourth). Keats uses a Spenserian stanza form (i.e. eight iambic pentameters followed by an alexandrine) for 'The Eve of St Agnes', and the eight-lined (*ottava rima*) form for 'Isabella'.

Summaries and textual notes on poems and letters

Extract from **I stood tip-toe upon a little hill**

In this poem, Keats tells the story of Endymion, later to be treated much more fully in the long poem of that name. Note here the easy use of run-on couplets, the sensitive appraisal of the scene in general and, in detail, the occasional descents into 'poetic' language. Balancing this last is a mastery of image rare in an early poem. The use of the couplet is interesting, the fluency prefiguring the maturity in handling the form later in 'Lamia'.

Nature's Common personification, inherited from 18th-century practice.

than ring-dove's cooings The wood-pigeon. A favourite Keats' image, occurring again in, for example, 'The Eve of St Agnes'.

sallows Willow trees (Latin *salix*). Cf the usage in 'To Autumn'.

chequer'd Variegated, breaking the uniformity of.

you might read two sonnets Conversational aside, something of a descent, but certainly indicative of Keats's own interests.

A natural sermon ... De Selincourt finds a reminiscence of *As You Like It* (Act II, Scene 1) – but echoes of Shakespeare and Milton (as well as of Leigh Hunt) are frequent in Keats at this stage.

Staying their wavy bodies ... Perhaps the best word for 'staying' here is 'bracing'.

ever wrestle ... ever nestle Keats becomes a master of the effective repetition (see 'Hyperion'), but here the usage is bathetic.

scantily Unusually, here this means 'briefly'.

right glad ... em'rald tresses Both clichés, the first commonplace, the second 'poetic'.

Like good men in the truth of their behaviours Keats seems to be striving for effect, the effect of 'integrity' or something like it, but the phrase is forced, clumsy.

a wanton freak i.e. a sudden impulse.

To Charles Cowden Clarke

This letter shows a strong literary awareness, a somewhat adulatory attitude towards Leigh Hunt (see note below), an inability to spell and a marked ability, which was never to desert him, to be at once conversationally interesting, colloquial and sensitive.

Charles Cowden Clarke The son of the headmaster of Clarke's School, where Keats was educated, he provided Keats with the early cultural friendship and encouragement which he needed. Clarke (1787–1877), later came to be celebrated for his knowledge of Shakespeare.

Mr Hunt Leigh Hunt (1784–1859), essayist and minor poet, editor of *The Examiner*, a major early influence on Keats. He was, at one time, imprisoned for his views, much to Keats's disgust.

Era Possibly Keats means an 'epoch'.

the Sonnet to the Sun See *RG*'s note on this.

Shakespeare and Darwin i.e. the major poet and the minor – the Darwin referred to being a physician and minor 18th-century poet (1731–1802), and the grandfather of Charles Darwin, the great English naturalist.

G. Mathew George Feeton Mathew, a friend and fellow poet.

Horace The great Roman poet (65–8 BC), who wrote odes, satires and epistles.

a Meeting i.e. a chapel.

a Charity which as St Paul saith See 1 Corinthians, 13, 13.

'On First Looking into Chapman's Homer'

Written in October 1816 after reading some of Chapman's translation of Homer's *Iliad* and *Odyssey*. (There is a full account of the composition of this small masterpiece in Robert Gittings's biography of Keats: *John Keats*, Heinemann, 1968, Chapter 6.) The few revisions are particularly important, and the error (Balboa, not Cortez, discovered the Pacific in 1513), is unimportant beside the imaginative sweep and maturity of expression to be found thus early in Keats's writing. The sonnet form was to exercise a major fascination on him (witness the number in the selection), and here the Elizabethan translator of Homer has fired him, the octave reflecting the inspirational force and extending it, so to speak, in the sestet through the cosmic and geographical associations. The kingdom of the imagination is thus harmonized with those other worlds of science (a new planet) and practical discoveries (a new sea), and this harmony is reflected in the command of language, of technical rhyme and form, of consonance and alliterative effects, of the ability to sustain metaphor and simile and excite the reader's wonder at the 'discovery' of Keats's own power and richness of expression.

the realms of gold i.e. of classical literature.

western islands i.e. Greek literature and culture.

in fealty i.e. in faithful service to (Apollo).

Apollo Son of Zeus, brother of Artemis, and god of medicine, music, poetry, archery, prophecy, light and youth.

demesne State, territory (to continue the metaphor).

pure serene Tranquillity.

Chapman George (1559–1634). Poet and playwright. De Selincourt points out that Chapman's translation of Homer appears to have influenced Keats throughout his writing career.

a new planet Probably the discovery of Uranus in 1781 by Sir (Frederick) William Herschel (1738–1882).

stout Cortez As indicated above, the reference should be to Balboa. Hernando Cortés (1485–1547) conquered Mexico and captured the Aztec emperor Montezuma, and later discovered California in 1535.

Darien The gulf of Darien on the Pacific.

Keen, fitful gusts

There is nothing of the elevation of the previous poem in the octave, but there is a fine contrast between the actuality of the walk and the carrying over of the warmth and the literary sympathies encountered at Hunt's cottage into the sestet. The form is exactly the same as that in the previous sonnet, the sestet with its alternate rhymes running into a completeness of expression, cumulative rather than end-stopped.

Keen, fitful gusts ... Note the simplicity of language in the octave, appropriate in view of the essential simplicity of the walk.

silver lamps Cliché for 'the stars'.

Milton's John Milton (1608–74), the author of *Paradise Lost* and of the wonderful elegy *Lycidas*. The subject of the poem was a minor poet called Edward King.

Laura ... faithful Petrarch Petrarch (1304–74), celebrated Italian lyric poet, wrote sonnets in praise of the surpassing beauty of Laura, who died in 1348.

To my brothers

The key here seems to be the word 'quietly', which indicates the meditative mood of the poet, his wish to weigh 'What are this world's true joys'. Again the form and structure is exactly the same as in the two preceding sonnets, but the tone, apart from one or two poetic phrases, is conversational throughout.

household gods i.e. 'the spirit of home, of the hearth'.

fraternal souls An obvious reference to his brothers.

Upon the lore i.e. the inward, meditative life.

aye Always.

ere the great voice i.e. of death.

To Haydon

This poem, to Keats's friend Haydon, includes references to Leigh Hunt and to Wordsworth: Haydon's painting *The Entry of Christ into Jerusalem* includes Keats and Wordsworth. Again the form of the sonnet is the same, but the innovation occurs in the thirteenth line, a half-line where the silence registers, or is meant to register without words, the impact of the 'Great spirits'. The tone is both elevated and specific in its reference to the poets and the painter.

Great spirits Wordsworth, Leigh Hunt and Benjamin Robert Haydon. Haydon (1786–1846) painted a number of important portraits of scenes from history (*Napoleon at St Helena*, for example), and devoted much energy to urging the acquisition, for this country, of the Elgin Marbles – so called because they were acquired by Lord Elgin.

Who on Helvellyn's summit Haydon's painting *Wordsworth Musing Upon Helvellyn* is in the National Portrait Gallery. Helvellyn is in the Lake District.

the chain for Freedom's sake A reference to Leigh Hunt's imprisonment.

Raphael's whispering A reference to the celebrated painter, sculptor and architect (1483–1520).

another heart The emphasis is on humanity and the imagination.

Of mighty workings i.e. not of the industrial age, but of the imagination.

On the Grasshopper and the Cricket

This sonnet, written to a pattern similar to that of the preceding ones, has an ease and fluency that gives perfect expression to the continuity and interlinkings of nature. The language throughout is as simple, as direct as the nature it describes.

To John Hamilton Reynolds, 17 April 1817

Reynolds (1794–1852) was a good if later a possessive friend to Keats, eventually turning from literature to the law; he will be known by a few as an effective parodist of Wordsworth. Carisbrooke is a village on the Isle of Wight where Keats was staying; its ruined castle once housed Charles I, executed in 1649, for thirteen months before his trial. The letter is charming and full of infectious enthusiasm, both for what Keats is doing and for what he has seen. It combines a rich and imaginative appraisal of the nature around him with a feeling for associations of the past, all imbued with Keats's own delightful, rambling 'conceits' and whimsy. In this there are some humorous and human admissions ('I did not feel very sorry at the idea of the Women being a little profligate'), the warmth of friendship ('a sketch of you and Tom and George . . .') and perhaps mockery of the dialect ('narvus').

Mary Queen (of) Scotts, and Milton Presumably sketches of the ill-fated Queen and of the English poet.

Shanklin Famous resort on the Isle of Wight. Keats estimates that it would cost him 'twice the expense' if he stayed there rather than at Carisbrooke.

The Keep The tower, stronghold.

Cowes to Newport Towns on the Isle of Wight.

being a little profligate i.e. because of the presence of the troops.

Fairy i.e. a spirit.

narvus nervous.

Do you not hear the Sea The actual words are Edgar's (Act IV, Scene 6 line 5) 'Hark! do you hear the sea?'

On the Sea

This is in the same form as 'On First Looking Into Chapman's Homer', but there is little or no elevation in the treatment. The idea of 'eternal whisperings' and the use of the word 'shores' is common in Keats, but the imaginative treatment is to be found in the fine sense of contrast between the sea's mightiest and minutest effects. The sestet opens with an invocation, commonplace rather than inspired, and the four 'ye's hardly raise the level of utterance. As we know, it was included in a letter to Reynolds, and while it is interesting in terms of Keats's feelings for the sea, poetically it is somewhat flat.

dinn'd with uproar rude The actual noise of the sea is cleverly captured in a succession of onomatopoeic consonants.

quired i.e. sang.

Extracts from Endymion, Book 1

This poem was begun in May 1817, and shows the influence of Leigh Hunt and Spenser; the rhyming couplets are run on and fluid. The poem was published in 1818 and attacked in two influential magazines of the time, *Blackwood's* and the *Quarterly Review*. After Keats's death there was a tendency to blame these and other reviews for hastening it ('Who killed John Keats?/I said the Quarterly/... 'Twas one of my feats', wrote Byron), but there is no reason to make this kind of connection. The whole of this allegorical poem deals with the love of the moon goddess for Endymion, the shepherd boy.

Lines 232–306 Each of the five 'paragraphs-in-verse' here is devoted to an invocation to the god Pan, the first being largely given to melancholy, the second to the sacrifices exacted from nature by the god, the third to a number of examples of the god's power and of his delight in it; the fourth verse stresses the protective nature of Pan and his mystical influence ('Leading to universal knowledge') while the fifth verse, the climax of the Hymn, further extols him and prays for his permanence. The interested student will read the poem as a whole, and then estimate the significance of these extracts in the light of it.

Eternal whispers Note the echoes of the sonnet we have just looked at.

hamadryads Nymphs of the trees.

Syrinx The nymph beloved and pursued by Pan; she was changed into a reed to escape him.

Passion Note the interesting, vital use of the word as a verb.

foredoom Have pledged.

girted Usually 'girded', meaning 'encircled'.

completions i.e. what has been fully ripened or produced.

faun and satyr The first rural deities with horns and tails, the second in human form with horses' ears and tails.

maw Stomach; but here appetite.

Naiads Nymphs of springs, rivers and lakes.

snouted ... routing Internal rhyme appropriate in a hymn.

minstrant Supplying, making (with a religious association).

Dread opener ... universal knowledge The implication is of mystical and supernatural powers, as befits a deity.

A firmament reflected in a sea A fine image to indicate the influence of Pan, and indeed of all imaginative greatness.

Paean The Greek choral lyric, sometimes accompanied by dancing.

Lycean Lycaeus is a mountain in Arcadia; the term is applied to Zeus.

Lines 777–842 This extract is a finely sustained meditation in which the poet relates happiness to love, passing through the various phases of delight in nature and history and imaginative experience to 'an orbed drop/Of light, and that is love' (lines 806–7). By this, says Keats, 'we are nurtured like a pelican brood' (line 815), and even those with latent greatness within them (Mark Antony is much in his mind) are ruled by this 'ardent listlessness' which he places at the centre and birth of all things. One may add here in commentary that this extract anticipates much of what Keats was to say again with increased maturity, but the effect here is of a questing mind and a rich and sensuous imagination.

becks i.e. beckons.

alchemiz'd Transmuted.

hist An interjection which calls attention to something.

Eolian From Aeolus, the god of winds.

Apollo's See note p.16.

clarions ... bruit Narrow-tubed trumpets ... spread aloud.

Orpheus The legendary pre-Homeric poet who mesmerized animals as well as humans with his playing of the lyre.

entanglements, enthralments Again, the choice of words is poor, bathetic.

genders i.e. engenders.

Melting into its radiance, we blend An image later to be used with specific intensity in *The Eve of St Agnes*.

wingedly Completely, imaginatively.

like a pelican brood The simile marks the movement from the ethereal to the factual – Pelicans are said to feed their young on their own blood.

tower'd in the van i.e. been prominent, foremost.

winnow ... chaff Note the running on of the image.

elysium The abode of the blessed after death, but here a state of ideal happiness.

ardent listlessness A superb paradox.

nightingale ... cloistered An anticipation in a few lines of what was the inspiration of the splendid ode.

bright mail The scales are like chain-mail.

dower Endowment, gift of nature.

runnels Brooks, rills.

its sweet Feeble phrase for 'fulfilment'.

To Fanny Keats, Wednesday, 10 Sept 1817

An interesting letter in that it includes a summary of *Endymion*, and indicates how hard at work Keats was on it while staying with Bailey in Oxford; it shows him, too, rather full of a somewhat naïve enthusiasm for it, and also for Oxford, but there is nevertheless an endearing tone about it.

his Whipship's Coach the Defiance A humorous knock at the coachman, and at the names of coaches.

Gothic The style of architecture, prevalent from the twelfth to sixteenth centuries, the pointed-arch style.

Lines rhymed in a Letter received (by J.H.R.) from Oxford

Three charming, light, six-lined verses, very much of the kind that Keats, so early in his career, was likely to include in a letter. The tone is humorous, mocking, somewhat irreverent and enjoyable.

Doric Simple, rustic. (Classical, Greek).

Crosier i.e. his pastoral staff.

Wilson the Hosier Keats has a keen sense of the ridiculous.
tassell trencher i.e. square college cap.
dominat i.e. he rules, lords it over everyone.
benison Blessing.

To Benjamin Bailey, Saturday, 22 Nov 1817

Bailey, born in 1791, went up to Oxford at the age of twenty-five to read for Holy Orders. He was a good influence on Keats at this time, urging him to read systematically. This is a most important letter, containing as it does much that Keats was to elaborate in his verse later, though here it is put with freshness and verve. Keats realizes the vastness of his subject in dilating upon genius, refers in passing to some brief unpleasantness between Haydon and Bailey, and then enumerates the following pivots of his own creed:

1 'What the imagination seizes as Beauty must be truth'.
   (The student should refer directly to the 'Ode on a
   Grecian Urn').
2 'The Imagination may be compared to Adam's dream.'
3 'O for a Life of Sensations rather than of Thoughts!'
4 'Imagination and its empyreal reflection is the same as
   human Life and its spiritual repetition.'

Later in the letter, No. 3, above, is qualified by the reflection that in the case of a complex 'Mind' the person is one 'who would exist partly on sensation partly on thought'. The letter is thus a considered assertion of belief, and that belief is reflected time and time again in the poems that are to come.

Men of Genius ... Men of Power Keats is fumbling towards a
   distinction which marks the 'Men of Genius' as people capable of
   flexibility and of infinite response towards experience, while 'Men
   of Power' have a 'determined Character' – that is, fixed.
3 vols octavo Keats is being satirical – the days of the 'three-
   decker' novel had begun, Scott's *Waverley* having been published
   in 1814.

Adam's dream This refers to Milton's *Paradise Lost* and not to Genesis. Briefly, Adam describes his dream of the birth of Eve, awaking to find, in Keats's words, 'Beauty is Truth'.

here after ... a finer tone and so repeated A belief in the immortality of the soul (for those 'who delight in sensation').

Imagination and its empyreal reflection ... Keats is equating the imaginative with the spiritual apprehension of 'Truth'.

Wine of Heaven ... redigestion Keats is putting to Bailey the idea that he should enjoy 'sensation' rather than 'hunger as you do after truth'.

Extract from *Endymion* Book 4, lines 512–48

This extract emphasizes the individual's capacity for depression at various levels and for various reaons; but the poet is optimistic about the comfort to be gained through the experience. Perhaps 'optimistic' is too strong a word to describe the onset of apathy, which is itself protection against the keener pangs of anguish and suffering. The depression moves through apathy to 'a dreamless sleep', a 'happy spirit-home' in the 'Cave of Quietude'. In the poem itself Endymion has just lost his 'human' love, the Indian maiden.

curtain'd bier The stand, suitably enclosed, on which the coffin or corpse is taken to the grave.

The death-watch tick i.e. the noise of the death-watch beetle.

Semele The mother of Dionysus; his father was Zeus.

Happy gloom! Note here and in the line further down the tendency to overdo the invocation.

Cave of Quietude i.e. of tranquillity, peacefulness.

Stanzas

Written in 1817, three simple verses of eight lines each, the first part of each verse having alternate lines rhyming followed by a triplet and a final line which rhymes with the final line of each of the succeeding verses (ababcccd). The theme is the passage of time, unfelt though registered externally in nature in the first two verses, contrasting with the sense of 'passed joy' in 'girl and boy' in the last verse. It is a poignant song, relying on subtle repetition and variation in the first two verses, and the contrast of the word-play in 'The feel of not to feel it' in the last.

drear-nighted Double-barrelled, and successfully evocative of atmosphere.

undo them Again evidence of advancing grasp of rhythm and rhyme: here the double rhyme maintains the personification of the tree.

stay their crystal fretting Fine image, perhaps meaning 'keep their pattern of ice'.

petting i.e. getting into a 'pet', or being worried.

Writh'd i.e. suffered acutely.

The feel ... feel An early instance of Keats's use of repetition to achieve economy of expression.

To George and Thomas Keats, Sunday, 21 Dec 1817

This letter contains Keats's definition of *Negative Capability* – 'of being in uncertainties, Mysteries, doubts, without any irritable reaching after fact and reason'. This he links, after citing Coleridge as an example of the opposite, with the idea that 'with a great poet the sense of Beauty overcomes every other consideration, or rather obliterates all consideration ...' These references further underline his deepening concern for his art, his strong ideal of vocation.

dovetailed i.e. came together, fitted together.

Penetralium Innermost recess.

To Mrs Reynolds's Cat

This sonnet was written at the beginning of 1818, and the form is – as usual with Keats at this time – each quatrain of the octave having a rhyming couplet between the two 'a' rhymes (abba abba); and alternate lines rhyming in the sestet (cdcdcd). It is a charming exercise, lightweight but with some fine descriptive touches.

Climacteric The critical period of life, the decline of the vital force.

segments Apt, unusual choice of descriptive word.

latent talons Again, a fine choice based on sensitive observation.

frays Fights, battles.

Asthma Again note the quality of Keats's observation.

the lists i.e. used in tournaments in the age of chivalry, particularly enclosing a tilting-ground.

glass-bottled wall i.e. glass built into the top of the wall to act as a deterrent against burglary.

On sitting down to read *King Lear* once again

Here the poet is turning his back on the temptations of 'Romance' – that is, his own somewhat self-indulgent writing – in order to submit himself to the conflicts and betrayals of *King Lear*, sufferings which are consonant to his own mood for the writing of 'Hyperion'. The date of composition is January 1818. It differs from the preceding sonnets by closing with all the finality – of self-discipline and determination – of a rhyming couplet.

Golden tongued Romance ... serene lute 'Escapist' writing, the lure of what the poet would like to do.

Syren ... Queen Note the heavy personification, part of Keats's invocatory style.

damnation and impassion'd clay Straight reference to a Shakespearean theme, and more specifically to *Lear*.

assay Attempt, try. (Often related to the purity of metals).

this Shakespearean fruit i.e. the play itself.

Albion The Greek and Roman name for Britain.

old oak Forest The phrase indicates endurance of like suffering to that which Shakespeare experienced.

new Phoenix wings A reference to the fact that the phoenix, mythological bird of the Arabian desert, was reputed to rise from the ashes of its funeral pyre. The image chosen by Keats is particularly appropriate in a poem on *Lear*, for the subject was treated by Shakespeare in 'The Phoenix and the Turtle'.

To George and Thomas Keats (Friday, 23 January 1818)

A letter rich in description, particularly of atmosphere ('greasy & oily'), with ironic and forthright touches, colloquial and vivid and with an engaging sense of involvement in what he does and sees. Here the 'sensations' are recorded unpoetically, but with the usual acute observation; the people and scenes come alive under Keats's touch.

a guttered Candle i.e. spent, played out.
Nota Bene Mark, note well.
the Green Room i.e. accommodating actors and actresses when they are off stage.
painted Trollop Slattern, tart.
in Mary A part in George Colman's comedy, *John Bull*.
habited as the Quaker Keats's irony at her 'let-down' of her part is apparent.
finger-point Rude gesture by a member of the audience.
dressed to kill i.e. to impress, flamboyantly.
the sweetest morsel i.e. the best or funniest thing (that happened).
boonsome Pothouse Presumably a kind of 'pub' music and routine.

When I Have Fears

Written in January 1818, and is in the Shakespearean form, i.e. three quatrains with alternate lines rhyming and climaxed by the couplet at the end of the poem. Keats mentions death throughout his poems (see 'Ode to A Nightingale' in particular), and the references are generally taken to refer to himself. Here the statement is overt, the first part of the poem rich in harvest and cosmic imagery, with the second part elevating the ephemeral experience to an importance greater than that of ambition.

glean'd my teeming brain i.e. set forth my many ideas.
charact'ry Hand-writing.
like rich garners The continuation of the harvest imagery.
Their shadows i.e. what they reflect and, perhaps, what they inspire.
fair creature See *RG*'s note; Keats has indicated the change of direction in his thoughts at the beginning of the sestet, thus reflecting his meticulous attention to structure.
have relish ... faery power Delight ... in the imaginative force.

Lines on the Mermaid Tavern

Written in 1818, this is a whimsical and essentially light treatment inspired by the Mermaid Tavern which was patronized by Shakespeare and Ben Jonson among others. The mood is reflected in the rhymed eight-syllabled couplets, the refrain being repeated at the end of the poem. The fluency, the imaginative flair, the whimsical 'conceit' (something of Elizabethan influence here, perhaps) make this a happy and attractive poem, surprisingly mature in execution.

fruits of Paradise i.e. Heaven.
bowse The 18th century word which became 'booze', drink much.
astrologer i.e. he 'saw' (Shakespeare, Jonson etc) in the 'stars' and set down what he saw – that they were still enjoying themselves, as of old, in the Heavens (the Zodiac).

To John Hamilton Reynolds, Thursday, 19 February 1818

This is a letter steeped in the contemplation of literature and its associations and influences, and is typical of Keats's imaginative writing – his mind plays with associations, and leads us on through a succession of vivid images.

delicious diligent Indolence Even here, a sense of alliterative music.

an odd angle of the Isle *The Tempest* (I, 2, 223). The speaker is Ariel, making his 'report' to Prospero.

a girdle round the earth *A Midsummer's Night's Dream* (II, 2, 175), Puck's reply to Oberon.

sparing touch i.e. brief look, acquaintance.

like the Spider A fine simile which Keats elaborates as he goes on.

Minds would leave each other If the previous lines in this letter are studied intently, it will become clear that Keats is arguing that we all experience and interpret works (here, pages) of literature differently, but that the sum total of responses is a coming together, an exchange, and therefore an enrichment.

a grand democracy of Forest Trees A fine mixed image to indicate the invaluable interchanges indicated above.

To John Taylor, Friday, 27 February 1818

The extract conveys the name and nature of Keats's thoughts on poetry, and is in itself an exquisite definition of them. Briefly summarized (though the interested reader will prefer Keats's own words to those given here) it means (a) that poetry should be a full expression and not a limited one; (b) that the reader should be so struck by the quality of the expression and meaning as to identify his own thoughts with them; (c) that the impact should be progressive and lead up to the fullness described; (d) that poetry should come naturally, unforced.

Extract from Isabella; or The Pot of Basil

Begun in February 1818, and finished before the end of April, though later perhaps revised. Keats's uneven use of *ottava rima*, an Italian stanza form which he may have regarded as agreeable with the source of the poem, means that each verse has a completeness which ends with the couplet and arrests narrative flow. The extract here shows Keats at his inspired best in terms of the range of the figurative associations, and at his bathetic worst in repetitious rhetorical questions. Rigg's translation of The *Decameron* has an admirable summary of the fifth story of the fourth day, which Keats adapted for 'Isabella':

Lisabetta's brothers slay her lover: he appears to her in a dream, and shews her where he is buried: she privily disinters the head, and sets it in a pot of basil, whereon she daily weeps a great while. The pot being taken from her by her brothers, she dies not long after.
(J. M. Rigg, *The Decameron of Boccaccio*, Navarre Society, N.D.)

Stanza 14
proud-quiver'd Note the force of the double-barrelled epithet. Note particularly in this verse the richness, the vividness of the word-pictures.

Stanza 15
Again the word-pictures, but here with a physical intensity and a strong humanitarian overtone.

Stanza 16
The bathos of this stanza has been variously noted. It is traceable to the repetition and the questions, mercifully unanswered, and also a slackness in construction – why should 'Half-ignorant' men have anything to do with the 'songs of Grecian years' anyway? Here the word-pictures are lacking the sharp outlines of those in the previous two verses.

lazar stairs i.e. where the beggars are to be found.

red-lined accounts i.e. indicating the profits *not* debits, as in modern bank accounts.

Stanza 17

The hawks . . . the untired Phrases which underline their capacity to do business on more than one level.

Quick cat's paws i.e. quick to take advantage of. Cf the modern meaning of 'catspaw': someone used as another's tool, a 'stooge'.

wits in Spanish, Tuscan and Malay This could mean that they had a kind of doggerel humour in these languages, or equally that they had their 'wits' about them in all their dealings.

Stanza 18

ledger-men Simple coinage to underline their simple greed.

Egypt's pest The Plague.

every dealer fair The phrase carries its own irony – these are manifestly unfair dealers.

Stanza 19

A pause in the narrative and an invocation to Boccaccio – the kind of intervention which was later to characterize certain writers of 19th century fiction (Thackeray in *Vanity Fair*, for example, or George Eliot in *Adam Bede*). It contributes nothing to the narrative here, and lowers the poetic quality.

ghittern's tune A reference to an old instrument of the guitar kind strung with wire (more commonly spelt 'gittern').

Stanza 20

meet Fitting.

gone spirit Dead, departed.

stead thee i.e. to speak instead of you.

Stanza 21

That he i.e. Lorenzo.

Stanza 22

cruel clay/Cut Mercy with a sharp knife to the bone Finely connected, and as suddenly physical and frightful as the murder to come.

and there bury him Notice the superb economy of the statement – as simple and effective as the killing.

Stanza 23

Notice how the spoken words, though conveying the hypocrisy, indicate a slackness in the narrative texture.

Stanza 24

Apennine i.e. the mountain range.

'His dewy rosary on the eglantine' The religious tone of the phrase is made the more ironic by the irreligious nature of what they are contemplating.

serpents' whine M. R. Ridley considers this term inappropriate to the brothers' attitude and status.

Stanza 25

There is a word-picture at the end of the verse, but the language is for the most part trite.

Stanza 26

'Ah! what if I should lose thee An unconscious anticipation of his own death.

Stanza 27

their murder'd man An anticipatory, prophetic epithet finely conveys Lorenzo's fate.

against the freshets Note the break in the line which enables Keats to move from the natural scene to the evidence of the *unnatural* act about to be perpetrated.

quiet for the slaughter The phrase, somewhat bathetic, indicates, in this instance, what can be the limitations of the *ottava rima* stanza, with its necessity for a concluding couplet.

Stanza 28

As the break-covert blood-hounds Breaking out of hiding.

Each richer Bathetic, as in the 'Why were they proud' verse.

To John Hamilton Reynolds, Sunday, 3 May 1818

In this letter Keats focuses on Wordsworth, and on his (own) conception of life. He describes a 'large Mansion of Many Apartments', and then proceeds to define them – the first being infancy, the second, with the onset of the 'thinking principle', the 'Chamber of Maiden-Thought'. At first all is delight here; this gives way to a darkening of the feelings, what Keats, using Wordsworth's phrase from 'Tintern Abbey', calls the 'burden of the Mystery'. Wordsworth is adept at exploring 'those dark Passages'. Here, says Keats, he has the advantage over Milton, who can be readily understood, particularly when one remembers the times in which he wrote. The chief difference is that Milton accepted the 'Dogmas' of his religion, whereas Wordsworth thought 'into the human heart'. Keats's conclusion is that 'there is really a grand march of intellect – It proves that a mighty providence subdues the mightiest Minds to the service of the time being, whether it be in human Knowledge or Religion.' Again one is forced to marvel at the maturity of expression and the sheer imaginative and rational perception of a young man who was not twenty-three years of age when he wrote this.

Wordsworth (1770–1850) Keats's great contemporary, who – in his preface to the *Lyrical Ballads* (1798) – together with Coleridge, had virtually initiated the Romantic movement in England.

Mansion of Many Apartments This appears to be a deliberate Biblical echo.

the burden of the Mystery ('Of all this unintelligible world') from Wordsworth's 'Lines Written Above Tintern Abbey'.

Milton (1608–74) See Note p.17.

a great superstition i.e. Catholicism.

Comus A masque (1634). The theme is as defined here by Keats.

Cod-pieces Bagged appendages to the front of the close-fitting hose or breeches worn by men, from the fifteenth to the seventeenth century.

the inquisition and burning at Smithfield The Roman
  Catholic tribunals for the suppression of heresy. Smithfield was
  the London centre for the burning of heretics.

To Thomas Keats, Saturday, 27 June 1818

An easy, unforced letter describing a visit to Wordsworth; it
is full of bright, natural observation and an exultation, as one
might expect, in the sheer beauty and 'difference' of the Lake
District scenery. Keats's delight is seen in his imaginative
associations with what he observes – 'like an arrow', 'like a
fan'. He is so impressed with the magnitude and colour of what
he sees that he takes issue with Hazlitt, who felt that 'these
scenes make man appear little'. On the contrary, says Keats,
'I never forgot my stature so completely.'

I live in the eye An economical and effective way of indicating
  his response to visual 'sensations' and stimulus.

Old Meg

Written in July 1818: the form, with the exception of the final
six-lined verse, is that of a ballad, the quatrains each having
the second and fourth lines rhyming. The popularity of the
poem is easily understood, for the pathos is immediate, the
natural description somehow ennobling as well as poignant.
Based on a fiction, it has an underlying realism: the simplicity,
the repetitions of the verses stress the monotony of poverty, as
well as its simple pleasures. But the form is such that we see the
symbol as the truth, and the comparisons in the final verse add
to the ennobling quality of this ballad.

chip hat A hat made from 'chips' – wood split into strips.

Lines Written in the Highlands after a Visit to Burns's Country

This is the description of a journey in a somewhat 'tramping' rhythm, entertaining but undistinguished, though it does show Keats as the master of a kind of informal verse, with plenty of natural observation and inward and imaginative reactions, as ever, both to what he sees and what he doesn't see. There is throughout an intense sense of the past, reactions to visions and fears, ending with the assertion that man must 'keep his vision clear from speck, his inward sight unblind'.

Druids Priests and soothsayers among the Celts of ancient Gaul and Britain.
unshorn i.e. without losing (his fame).
Runnels Brooks, rills.
high-cedar'd Fine double-barrelled epithet.
Palmer's i.e a pilgrim's.
a Bard's A poet's.
bourn Small stream, boundary.
pain a painter's Keats is guilty here of word-play that fails to enhance the image.

To Thomas Keats, Sunday, 26 July 1818

Largely a description of his reactions in the Western Highlands, with a vivid, and very imaginative, account of Fingal's Cave. Keats expresses something of religious awe in face of these sights.

Staffa Island near Mull in the Inner Hebrides, off the Atlantic coast of Scotland.
Fingal's Cave The basaltic cavern of Staffa, named after the legendary Gaelic hero.
Jove Jupiter, the chief of the gods.
Iona The island off the tip of Mull, associated with St Columba and the coming of Christianity to Scotland.

Hyperion, a fragment, Book 1

Written 1818–19: it had been in Keats's mind for some time, perhaps being originally seen as 'a companion poem to 'Endymion', and in the latter there are hints about its future composition. The preface to *Endymion* is even more explicit, where he refers to 'the beautiful mythology of Greece', and says of it that, 'I wish to try once more.' Probably Book 3 of the work was written after his brother Tom's death, and it seems unlikely that he added any more to it after April 1819. In September he wrote to Reynolds 'I have given up *Hyperion*'.

It is quite obvious that there were a number of literary influences on Keats – Chapman's translation already referred to, Keats's own reading in Spenser and in Milton (particularly, of course, *Paradise Lost*) and translations too of Ovid. According to De Selincourt in his instructive notes on the poem, Keats confuses giants and Titans, as well as the Greek and Latin names of characters mentioned. Be that as it may, the fragment as it stands is worthy of a full critical consideration, for even allowing for confusions it is a remarkable and independent work. In the first Book the revolt against the Titans has begun, and Saturn and Oceanus have already been overcome, and many of their contemporaries chained. Hyperion's realm is already under threat. The 357 lines of Book 1 (slightly under half the length of Book 1 of *Paradise Lost*) comprise an unforgettable picture of the fallen Saturn, visited by Thea, Hyperion's wife, who has come to summon him to the Council of the Titans. This is followed by an equally impressive picture of Hyperion himself, who, although he knows of his forthcoming fate, determines to offer mighty resistance. In this he is encouraged by his father Coelus, who expresses pity for him but little more than that, and the book ends with Hyperion plunging into darkness to join his fellow-Titans. The opening of Book 2 (a direct Miltonic parallel here) presents the Titans in council; Saturn has now come to them, and listens to Oceanus and his account of their fated fall. He speaks particularly of the beauty of the young god who has overcome him, and this is largely echoed in Clymene's account of the transcendent brightness of Apollo. This side of the debate is balanced, however, by the words of Enceladus, who soundly berates them for their lack of courage and calls upon them to resist, pointing out that they have a natural leader in Hyperion, the sun-god, who is not yet disgraced as they are. But when Hyperion arrives, his dejection, his own sense of coming doom, is quickly communicated to the other Titans.

Book 3 tells of the meeting between Apollo and Mnemosyne, but just as Apollo reaches the divinity which will make him all-powerful, the poem breaks off. Much conjecture has been spent on how the poem would have ended had Keats proceeded with it. His publishers said that he was discouraged from so doing by the 'reception' given to *Endymion*, but this is unlikely. This is not the place to attempt a full-scale critical appreciation of the poem, for the textual notes below are intended specifically as the main critical guide, but it is perhaps appropriate to indicate here that 'Hyperion' represents what De Selincourt calls 'the height of Milton's influence upon Keats'. The latter came to feel with successive re-readings that *Paradise Lost* was ever 'a greater wonder' to him. One feels that sometimes consciously and at other times unconsciously Keats imitated Miltonic effects – the epic similes, the language of debate, the inverted word-order, for example – and De Selincourt lists a number of similarities and derivations, such as classical constructions, repetitions, vocabulary, intonations. Keats himself testifies to the fact that he considered the poem too heavily dependent on Milton, but it has an abundance of Keatsian individuality too, and the careful reader of the poem will be aware of this even as he reads. As Shelley remarked, 'The great proportion of this piece is surely in the very highest style of poetry.'

Book 1 (The form throughout the poem is blank verse.)

2–3 **Far ... Far from** One of Milton's – and Keats's – favourite devices: simple, sometimes cumulative, repetition.
Saturn Chronus, or Kronos (Time).

4 **quiet as a stone** Effective short simile.

6 **Forest on forest ... like cloud on cloud** See the note on repetition above; the effect here is rhetorical.

11 **A stream went voiceless by** Superb evocation of atmosphere – the effects of *silence*.

18 **nerveless, listless, dead** Note the resonant effect of the single words, with each of the first two negative, the third irrevocably positive. This is continued in the next line.

27 **By her in stature** The intonation is Miltonic, as is the classical elaboration which extends to line 33. The 'one' is Thea, wife to Hyperion.
Amazon According to Greek legend, a warlike race of women in Asia Minor.

29 **Achilles** Son of Peleus and Thetis, chief hero on the Greek side in the Trojan war.

30 **Ixion's wheel** A king bound to a revolving wheel of fire for his impiety in trying to imitate the thunder of heaven. (Another version of the myth is that the king was punished for trying to seduce Hera.)

31 **Memphian sphinx** A large Egyptian sculptured Sphinx was on exhibition in London at the time of Keats's writing.

33 **sages** Wise men.
lore Traditions, doctrines.

35 **if sorrow had not made** Again the balance of the repetition for emphasis of the outstanding trait or effect.

67 **'That unbelief has not a space to breathe'** i.e. That not for a moment can what has happened be doubted.

72 **As when** A fine simile again evocative of silence, but conveying the essential peacefulness and dignity of nature, almost like an unfallen god.
tranced Entranced.

73–4 **green-rob'd ... branch-charmed** Fine double-barrelled epithets which reflect the dignity and the mysterious romance of the comparison.

84 **Her silver seasons four** Note the Miltonic inversion of the construction.

86 **Like natural sculpture in cathedral cavern** Look back to Keats's description of Fingal's cave.

129 **metropolitan** Mother country.

137 **Druid** See note p.35.

145 **Chaos** The formless void.

146 **Olympus** The home of the Gods.

147 **The rebel three** Zeus, Poseidon and Dis (Roman equivalents, Jupiter, Neptune and Pluto).

154 **the shade** The gloom.

156–7 **mist ... nest** A half-rhyme rounding off a blank verse paragraph.

161 **The Titans** Strictly, the gigantic race, children of Uranus and Ge (Heaven and Earth).

173 **the first toll** i.e. signifying death.

175 **portion'd to** i.e. proportionate to.

181 **Aurorian** Dawn-like, after Aurora (Eos in Greek), goddess of dawn.

197 **minions** Servants.

198 **like anxious men** Fine Miltonic simile – underlining the feelings, and hence the sufferings, of gods and men alike.

207 **Zephyrs** The nymphs of the west wind.

209 **like a rose** Again a superb natural simile.

213 **He enter'd** But note the qualification of this which comes straight afterwards, and makes Hyperion immediately impressive.

231 **'Why do I know ye?'** Note the rhythmic variation, as arresting to the reader is as Hyperion's presence to the fallen Titans.

238 **pure fanes** i.e. temples.

246 **Tellus** In Roman religion, the Divinity of the Earth.

253 **For as in theatres** Again the Miltonic tone is apparent.

274 **colure** One of two great circles intersecting rectangularly at the poles and dividing equinoctial and ecliptic into four equal parts.

276 **nadir** i.e. the deepest point.

302 **And all along a dismal rack of clouds** This is the portent of Hyperion's doom, but the word-pictures of the previous forty or so lines are a vivid evocation of his power.

307 **Coelus** Father of Saturn.

326 **Pale wox I** (De Selincourt has *was* for *wox*).

328 **must unlike Gods** A misprint for 'most'.

343 **in the van/Of Circumstance** i.e. Coelus's advice is 'act first – act while you can'.

355 **Like to a diver ... all noiseless** Note the effectiveness of the simile and the reminiscence of *Isabella*: For them the Ceylon diver held his breath/And went *all* naked ...

Book 2

4 **Cybele** Goddess of the powers of nature, said by some to be Saturn's wife.

19–20 **Coeus, and Gyges, and Briareüs/Typhon, and Dolor and Porphyrion** The first is 'one of the Titans', the second and third were born to Uranus and Ge, Typhon appears to be Enceladus, while Dolor and Porphyrion are difficult to identify. Keats is, however, employing a favourite Miltonic device of 'listing' names in an impressive and rhetorical way.

29 **Mnemosyne** The mother of the Muses by Zeus (Jupiter).

30 **Phoebe** Daughter of Uranus and Ge.

34 **like a dismal cirque** Fine image, apparently suggested by the Druid stones near Keswick.

41 **Creus** one of the Titans.

44 **Iapetus** Married to Asia (see below).

49 **Cottus** Apparently, according to Hesiod, of later birth than the other Titans.

53 **Asia** Daughter of Oceanus and Tethys. She is usually identified with Clymene.
Caf In the Mohammedan faith Kaf is held to be a fabulous mountain, so Keats is here making his own mythology for Asia.

60 **By Oxus or in Ganges' sacred isles** Here again there is a Miltonic geographical width about the reference. The first is

the river in Asia called now the Amu Darya, the second the sacred river of India.

61 **Even as Hope** An unclassical simile, but the representation (seen later on Cape of Good Hope stamps) would be familiar enough in Keats's time.

66 **Enceladus** Typhon, the strongest of the Titans.

73 **Atlas** The son of Iapetus and Asia.

74 **Phorcus, the sire of Gorgons** A Greek sea-god. The Gorgon's head turned to stone anything that met its gaze.

77 **Themis** A Titan, mother of Prometheus.

78 **Ops** Rhea, goddess of the harvest.

86 **Above a sombre cliff** Note, looking closely here and elsewhere, how Keats subtly varies the break in the line to obtain the maximum emphasis.

95 **Remorse, spleen, hope** Again a fine rhetorical sequence of single-word effects.

97 **a mortal oil** i.e. He was now subject to fear and suffering.

138 **my firm-based footstool** i.e. on which I relied.

161 **how engine our great wrath** i.e. how can we fit ourselves, manage our anger.

165 **astonied** Astonished.

187 **eternal truth** The key to the passage, and in some ways to the poem: the eternal truth is that there is a cycle of change, and that the young, strong and beautiful will dispossess the old.

224 **We are such forest-trees** Note the fine command of rhetoric, and the range of natural reference in this speech.

228-9 **for 'tis the eternal law/That first in beauty should be first in might** The explicit expression of tacit acceptance of the rebellion and its effects.

245 **poz'd** i.e. affected, put on.

298-9 **this too indulged tongue/Presumptuous** Again the influence of Milton is evident here with the splitting of *indulged* and *Presumptuous* for emphasis.

328 **ether** The upper regions beyond the clouds.

358 **beetling** Overhanging.

371 **Numidian curl** Like the mane of a lion.

374 **Memnon** The son of Tithonus and Aurora. He was killed by

Achilles; he had a statue in the grove of Serapis, in Egyptian Thebes.

Book 3

3 **O leave them, Muse!** Marks a departure, for the phrase is repeated four lines further on and indicates a change of mood, a turning away to what Keats calls 'A solitary sorrow'.

10–12 **the Delphic harp ... Dorian flute** The first perhaps meaning 'mysterious', from the oracle at Delphi, the second meaning simple and solemn.

23 **Cyclades** A group of islands in the southern part of the Aegean Sea.

24 **Delos** One of the Cylades.

40 **Unhaunted by the murmurous noise of waves** Note how the syllabic content of the line, and the 's' sounds in particular, convey the movement of the sea.

50 **unfooted** A finely economical way of saying 'which cannot be walked on'.

82 **Mnemosyne** Mother of the Muses and goddess of memory.

119 **elixir** Here a potion to prolong life indefinitely.

To James Augustus Hessey, Thursday, 8 Oct 1818

A brave letter in which Keats argues that his own self-criticism has given him much more pain than the reviews of Endymion in *Blackwood* or the *Quarterly*. He takes the view that he has 'leaped headlong into the Sea' by writing *Endymion*, but that he has learned much from the experience and that he was 'never afraid of failure'. The key sentence in the letter, though perhaps general in purport, expresses his own belief in relation to himself, that 'poetry must work out its own salvation in a man'.

the Chronicle i.e. *The Morning Chronicle* Two letters were in fact published in the paper, on the 3rd and 8th October 1818, the first by J. S. (see below) and the second by R.B. The first in particular is an eloquent defence of *Endymion* and an attack on the reviewers.

Blackwood or the Quarterly Literary magazines and reviews.

In the first Keats had been attacked in an article called 'The Cockney School of Poets', and John Wilson Croker had written an abominable attack on him in the second.

J.S. Identified by some as John Scott (1783–1821).

Soundings i.e. testing the depths of.

nigh getting into a rant Close to making an exaggerated speech.

To George and Georgiana Keats, Wednesday, 14 October 1818

A letter in praise of a lady, John Hamilton Reynolds's cousin, Jane Cox. Her beauty greatly moved Keats, and this letter is an account of the meeting. See *RG* for an interesting note on the word 'particular'.

Charmian One of Cleopatra's attendants, the one in whom she confided chiefly.

because I live in her i.e. I give myself up purely to the pleasure she affords me.

a tune of Mozart's might do The celebrated composer (1756–91) born at Salzburg.

whose Lips is to me a banquet A reminiscence of *Macbeth* (I, 4), where Duncan observes to Banquo (ironically of Macbeth), 'He is full so valiant/And in his commendations I am fed. It is a banquet to me.'

To George and Georgiana Keats, 26 October 1818

Another letter in which Keats reveals his susceptibility to female beauty. It is a fascinating letter, showing Keats amused at his own motives; and it gives a graphic account of his responses, in an entirely unselfconscious and human way. There are moments of self-mockery too ('a sort of genteel hint from the Boarding School').

tasty Tastefully furnished.

Buonaparte i.e. Napoleon. At this time he would be exiled in St Helena.

aeolian Harp A stringed instrument producing musical sounds on exposure to the wind.

I thought it would be living backwards i.e. taking a backward step, not making the most of my opportunity.

libidinous i.e. licentious.

à peu près de mon age About my own age.

To Richard Woodhouse, Tuesday, 27 October 1818

Woodhouse came to have quite a lot to do with Keats, whom he met through Keats's publishers Taylor and Hessey. In this letter Keats tries to define the 'poetical Character' (it is not, as far as he is concerned, the 'egotistical sublime' of Wordsworth) – in his mind it is everything capable of experience, subject to change, hence the term 'camelion' poet, he has no self, no identity. He further speaks of himself as being 'annihilated' in company. The last paragraph expresses Keats's determination to 'reach to as high a summit in Poetry as the nerve bestowed upon me will suffer'. Again, this is a very important letter in showing us Keats's attitude towards poetry and, indeed, towards life.

egotistical sublime i.e. concern with self, but raised to an elevated level.

per se Intrinsically.

Iago as an Imogen The first the villain of *Othello*, the second Cymbeline's tender and artless daughter in Shakespeare's *Cymbeline*.

saturn and Ops See notes on *Hyperion* Book II.

then not myself goes home to myself i.e. I do not *live* in myself but in the lives of those around me.

I am sure however Notice the delicate way Keats turns from his uncertainty of identity on the poetic level to a courteous assurance on the human one.

To George and Georgiana Keats, Friday 18 Dec 1818

The extract here describes Fanny Brawne (see the section on

The author and his work), with whom Keats fell in love. The tone of the letter is humorous in parts, almost as if Keats is (a) perhaps not revealing his feelings and (b) mocking the idea of reporting on somebody to a third party. Consequently there is a balance between negatives and half-compliments.

wants Lacks.
a little painful Too delicate.

Ode: Bards of Passion and Of Mirth

This marks a return to the octosyllabic couplets of 'Lines on the Mermaid Tavern'. It was written in December 1818, 'a sort of Rondeau' though called an ode. The subject is what he called the 'double immortality' of poets. This is the after-life of Keats's fancy, the poets in the 'elysium' posited in 'Lines on the Mermaid Tavern', and the poems they have left on earth that continue to speak for them. Once again the mastery of the form is evident, and the fanciful treatment underlines a serious concern for the survival of poetry.

parle i.e. talk, conversation.
Dian's fawns i.e. belonging to the Goddess of the Moon.
Not a senseless, tranced thing But compare with the 'Ode to a Nightingale'.
Wisdom, though fled far away Keats's idea is that poetic experience – lack of identity but expressive of change, response, suffering, ecstasy – is in itself a kind of wisdom.
Double-lived in regions new! The repetition of the four lines at the end constitutes a reiteration of the main theme.

'Fancy'

This delightful poem was written at about the same time, and in the same form as the one above, Fancy being equated with the imagination. Firstly we are taken on a romp through the seasons, and then the scene is set by a winter's fire, with imagination able to supply there and then all the seasons and their particular richness; once imagination has kindled 'these pleasures up' the poem becomes a superb, lyrical expression of nature's beauties, imbued with acute observation and sense impressions. The final verse-paragraph suggests that imagination has much more to give us than reality, where 'Every thing is spoiled by use'. There is a fine use of the refrain, while the sensual indulgence of this last section asserts that an ideal love is better than a real one. Again, despite the lightness of touch, the poem has a serious undercurrent – life changes and dies, imagination lives.

by the ingle i.e. the nook, the chimney-corner.
sear Dry.
shoon Archaic for 'shoes'.
sward Lawnlike ground.
Ceres' daughter Ceres was the Roman name of Mother Earth, and her daughter was Persephone (or Proserpine).
the God of Torment Pluto.
Hebe's Daughter of Zeus and Hera, the handmaiden of the Gods.

The Eve of St Agnes

This is Keats's most visual of poems. It was begun at Chichester towards the end of January 1819, and finished after Keats had returned to Hampstead in February. He was obviously influenced by Chatterton in seeking a subject in medieval legend, and in the form in which he chose to express it the guiding hand is that of Spenser. The latter influenced the manner, the imagery and the metre, the alexandrine which closes each verse being a direct reminiscence of the *Faerie Queene*. If Keats owes to Spenser the sense of chivalry, the idealization of womanhood seen in Madeline, then the cumulative contrasts, the atmosphere of wonder on the one hand and the coldness on the other, are all his own. The sensuous qualities, too, have reached a new maturity of expression here, and the contrast of age and youth, impotence and virility, is finely captured.

The spell works for us as it works for Porphyro and Madeline, and the individual coinages, the succession of word-pictures, the feeling that 'Beauty' is 'truth', the mastery of the chosen form – all these cohere to make our experience in reading the poem a permanently vibrant one. Whereas the *ottava rima* of *Isabella* unfortunately lent itself to false rhetoric and bathos, the nine-lined verses here allow both for the visual focus, the details of the picture, the ongoing sweep of the imagination *and* the maintenance of the tension in the narrative. St Agnes' Eve is 20 January, and the idea of the legend (which is fully explained in the poem) may have come from Keats's reading of Burton's *Anatomy of Melancholy*.

Stanza 1
The owl. Note the fine evocation of an atmosphere of intense cold through nature, a telling contrast with Madeline's room later.

the Beadsman's The old servant whose task was to say prayers on behalf of the family.
incense ... censer Note that the half-pun reflects a keen sense of the silent effect, the soft sounds of the words perfectly conveying movement but no noise.
Past the sweet Virgin's The alexandrine (twelve syllabled line) conveys the movement of his 'frosted breath'.

Stanza 2
meagre, barefoot, wan The single-word effects noticed in *Hyperion*, here with a flatness appropriate to the atmosphere.
seem to freeze Note the imaginative identification of this – a further underlining of the atmosphere.
orat'ries Oratories. Places of worship and prayer.

Stanza 3
already had his deathbell rung This appears to mean that his days were already numbered – he was doomed to die that night,

which he spent in prayer for others (the family), as we learn from the rest of this stanza.

Stanza 4

up aloft i.e. in the 'level chambers' referred to.

silver, snarling Fine, light onomatopoeic effect.

The carved angels Notice the exact, meticulous visual picture we are being given, enhanced by the imaginative *life* ('eager-eyed') breathed into what is inanimate.

Stanza 5

argent revelry Silver; perhaps a reference to the armorial bearings.

The brain ... of old romance This helps to give the 'dream' atmosphere which is so much a part of the poem.

Stanza 6

They told her how There follows the account of the legend.

the honey'd middle ... couch supine Already, thus early in the poem, the mixture of the lush and the sensuous is apparent; Keats is intent on preparing for the striking scene of Madeline's awakening.

Stanza 7

whim ... Madeline Again a half-rhyme contributes to the running melody of the poem.

Stanza 8

the timbrels Tambourines.

amort Dead to. (Keats's own coinage.)

her lambs unshorn Another visual reference – St Agnes often being represented with lambs in paintings (she was martyred at the age of thirteen).

Stanza 9

Porphyro, with heart on fire/For Madeline The situation is that of Romeo and Juliet, but without the 'ill-starred' tragedy to follow which besets Shakespeare's lovers.

Buttress'd from moonlight Again note the quality of the visual picture.

speak, kneel, touch, kiss Note again the single words, here forming a sequence which prefigures Porphyro's coming experience.

Stanza 10

beldame Old woman, hag.

Stanza 11

the whole blood-thirsty race! Though the reference is not specific, the echoes of the Montague-Capulet feud of *Romeo and Juliet* are apparent.

Stanza 12

bier See note p.24.

Stanza 13

Pale, lattic'd, chill ... tomb Note the fine contrast of the single words, and the ominous threat in the last word.

When they St. Agnes wool The wool woven by nuns for the archbishop's pall.

Stanza 14

in a witch's sieve i.e. you will need to work magic (to get out of this).

mickle Much.

Stanza 15

Like puzzled urchin Note the deliberate distortion in this simile, which sustains the dream-like quality and makes it more grotesque than life.

brook i.e. put up with, tolerate.

Stanza 16

Sudden a thought came like a full-blown rose An image which conveys both the idea (stratagem) and physical passion, however repressed that has to be. The image is extended sexually – and brilliantly – later.

stratagem Plan.

Stanza 17

ruffian passion i.e. sexual desire.

more fang'd than wolves and bears Like the 'serpents' whine' in 'Isabella', this image is bathetic rather than effective.

Stanza 18

passing-bell cf the Beadsman, and the underlining of the age-death, youth-life theme of the poem, a theme of course developed in 'Hyperion'.

plaining i.e. complaining.

betide her weal or woe Whether it brings her good fortune or bad.

Stanza 19

legion'd fairies … pale enchantment Again the reiteration of the dream-like, supernatural atmosphere in which the poem exists. We know that at one stage Keats wished to revise the conclusion to make it more realistic; this kind of description subserves romance.

Merlin paid his Demon Merlin, Celtic 'magician' of King Arthur's time, was called 'the Prince of Enchanters'. He 'paid his Demon' by his own death.

Stanza 20

cates and dainties i.e. the preparation of a feast, part of the legend which is of Keats's own making.

tambour frame Circular frame on which silk is stretched to be embroidered.

Stanza 21

espial Discovery.

silken, hush'd and chaste Note here the combination of the single words again to produce an atmosphere.

Stanza 22

mission'd spirit i.e. a spirit with a mission; again note the romantic, supernatural effect, splendidly conveyed by the economy of the epithet.

like ring-dove fray'd and fled i.e. like the dove, fearful and flown.

Stanza 23

Its little smoke, in pallid moonshine, died Apt natural observation, though perhaps based on one of Sir Walter Scott's anecdotes about Wordsworth telling of Crabbe's extinguishing just such a candle, not letting his imagination play on the gradual dying of the smoke.

voluble ... eloquence Keats is stressing the 'language' of the feelings.

As though a tongueless nightingale An imaginative 'truth' which conveys the tensions, the fears, the wonderment of Madeline.

Stanza 24

A casement high A fine descriptive sequence (for the source see *RG*), rich in imagination of the man-made and the natural, and intensely visual in its effects. In a sense its beauties are in direct contrast with the beauty we – and Porphyro – are about to see, that of Madeline.

Stanza 25

gules Blood-red.

amethyst Semi-precious stone, purple or violet in colour.

saint ... angel ... heaven ... free from mortal taint Note how the sequence emphasizes the spiritual qualities of Madeline, qualities which are to be immediately contrasted in the next verse with her actions, which, though innocent, are physical.

Stanza 26

warmed Note the immediate, physical effect of this word.

like a mermaid in sea-weed Again the image conveys the unconsciously seductive appearance of Madeline. The blending of the spiritual and the physical is one of the major triumphs of the poem.

Stanza 27

Soon ... shut Note the running 's' sounds in this verse, alliteratively suggestive of sleep.

missal ... Paynims Prayer book ... Mohammedans.

Stanza 28

as fear in a wide wilderness Notice how effective, how full of tension – the kind of tension known to us all – this is.

Stanza 29

Morphean amulet A charm to preserve sleep (so that Madeline will not awaken). Morpheus, of course, was the god of sleep.
Affray Disturb.

Stanza 30

azure-lidded Fine double-barrelled coinage.
soother *RG* says 'more soothing', from Chatterton.
argosy Large merchant vessels (Elizabethan associations here).
Fez Turkish town.
Samarcand ... Lebanon The first a town in the USSR, on the borders of Afghanistan, the second the republic on the Mediterranean between Jordan, Syria and Israel.

Stanza 31

retired quiet This juxtaposition of words gives a particular lilt to the verse.
eremite Hermit (dedicated to the service of God in the wilderness).

Stanza 32

entoil'd in woofed phantasies Caught up in dreams he is weaving.

Stanza 33

Tumultuous Note the single word again, this time conveying the nature of his feelings.
Provence i.e. in southern France, the home of the troubadours.
La belle dame sans mercy *RG* identifies the original author as Alain Chartier.
pale as smooth-sculptured stone Again the visual element predominates.

Stanza 34

so dreamingly Another example in this poem of a bathetic ending to the verse.

Stanza 35

pallid, chill and drear! Here the words contrast with the vibrant reality to come.

Stanza 36

Beyond a mortal man The whole verse is full of emotional and physical awakening, Porphyro's response being sexual, and the image of the rose and violet blending, of dream and reality coming together, is an anticipation of sexual consummation and the fulfilment of romantic love.

St. Agnes' moon hath set Note the superb climax to the verse, brief, direct, the legend fulfilled.

Stanza 37

A dove forlorn and lost The interested student will note that the bird imagery forms a unifying element throughout the poem.

Stanza 38

vassal Slave – a medieval, chivalric tone.

vermeil dyed Vermilion.

shrine ... pilgrim Note the return, after the 'passion', of the spiritual associations.

Stanza 39

bloated wassaillers Surfeited drinkers.

Rhenish German wine.

sleepy mead Fermented from honey, a heavy, sleep-inducing drink.

Stanza 40

dragons ... spears Mixed image, somewhat bathetic and loose.

arras Rich tapestry, often hung round the walls of rooms.

Stanza 41

an inmate i.e. an occupant of the house (Madeline).

the bolts i.e. of the door.

Stanza 42

coffin-worm A species of worm that eats into the coffin to get at the flesh.

aves Repeated prayers.

The Eve of St Mark

This was written in February 1819, and is in the octosyllabic couplets of 'Bards of Passion and of Mirth'. The connections with 'the Eve of St Agnes' and medieval legend are obvious, and *RG*'s note on the series of word-pictures is particularly interesting. St Mark's Eve is 24 April. The description of nature is precise throughout, as is that of the streets of the cathedral city.

aguish hills Perhaps 'shivering' is meant here.

half done i.e. half finished.

Aaron's breastplate See Exodus 28, 30.

the seven/Candlesticks John saw in Heaven See Revelations 1, 20.

Lion of St Mark This was in Venice.

Covenantal Ark ... golden mice See 1 Samuel, 6, 2–4.

And struck a lamp from the dismal coal There is rhythmic reflection of Coleridge's 'Christabel' here.

Lima mice Lemur mice. Keats is possibly referring here to lemurs – nocturnal mammals of the East (particularly Madagascar), allied to monkeys but with pointed muzzles.

Macaw Parrot.

Av'davat The amadavat, a bird of India.

eremite Hermit.

'Gif ye wol ... Of Saintè Markis life and dethe This is not genuine medieval language: roughly paraphrased, the words mean, 'If you stand in the church porch you will see people approach who are marked for death during the coming year. The book that Bertha is reading also tells of the birth of a child; the Virgin birth; the love of God, the power of evil, of St Cecilia and of the life and death of St Mark' De Selincourt considers that the influence here is Chatterton.

To George and Georgiana Keats, Friday, 19 March 1819

A letter of concern for his friend Haslam, who is awaiting the death of his father, but extending into themes which are present in the 'Ode on a Grecian Urn' and the 'Ode to Melancholy'. It is expressive too of involvement in Haslam's sufferings, with the corollary that 'our own touch us too nearly for words'. Throughout there is a running comparison between the ways of man and the ways of nature, for example in the getting of a mate and in comparable 'leisure'. It shows Keats's veneration for the great men Socrates and Jesus, and he feels that it can be said of each that 'though he transmitted no writing of his own to posterity, we have his Mind and his sayings and his greatness handed to us by others'.

Circumstances are like Clouds A fine image to indicate oppression.

seed of some trouble ... arable land of events ... sprouts ... poison fruit Even in a letter Keats displays a natural facility in fashioning a connected sequence of metaphors.

Socrates The Athenian philosopher pronounced by the Delphic oracle to be the wisest of men.

handed to us by others i.e. in the case of Jesus, the four gospels for example, and in the case of Socrates, Plato.

Bright Star (final version)

(For a stimulating piece of biographical detection, see Robert Gittings's *John Keats: The Living Year*, Chapter 3.) The language of this final version of the poem is exquisite, with a microcosmic sweep of vision, as well as a strongly sensual realism too. Thus the octave, which has alternate lines rhyming, has the permanence of the world and the heavens set beside the transitory nature of man's life and love; what is superb is the sense of perspective which sees the 'mask/Of snow upon the mountains and the moors' and the physical immediacy of being 'Pillow'd upon my fair love's ripening breast'. The stress is on the ephemeral, but the quality of life experience is finely conveyed, so that the death-wish is seen as an escape from what would suffer change anyway.

Eremite See note p.54.
priestlike i.e. because they are purifying the earth as the priest purifies the soul.
tender-taken The double-barrelled word is, of course, from the consciousness of the lover.

To George and Georgiana Keats, Friday, 16 April 1819

This is a letter describing Keats's reading of Dante and the delightful dream he had as a result – this he turns into the sonnet which follows – and he goes on to express the wish that he could always dream such a dream.

Dante Dante Alighieri (1265–1321) immortalized Beatrice through his verse. His *Divine Comedy* has always exerted a profound influence on other writers.

On A Dream

This is written in the same form as the 'Bright Star' sonnet, ending with a couplet (as in the Shakesperian sonnet). The classical parallel between Hermes and the poet's imagination is touched upon, but the journey of the imagination in the dream is not to the 'isles of Greece' but to Dante's second circle which is described in the letter. In that fifth canto of *Hell* Dante and Virgil descend from the first circle into the second, where the souls of the lustful are tossed forever. They see many famous lovers, and Francesca of Rimini tells her story. In the dream the poet actually becomes one of the lovers, for 'Pale were the lips I kissed, and fair the form.'

Hermes The messenger of the Gods.
Argus The fabulous creature with a hundred eyes who was killed by Hermes.

Delphic reed ... idle spright My spirit played a musical pipe.
Ida On Crete, where Zeus was brought up in a cave.
Tempe A valley in the north-east of Thessaly, celebrated as a
  haunt of Apollo and the Muses.

La Belle Dame Sans Merci

Written in April 1819. See RG's important note explaining
how H. F. Cary's translation of the *Divine Comedy* influenced
Keats in the use of blank verse. Note also the use of the
ballad form and the sustained feeling of desolation that comes
across, together with the medieval and supernatural
atmosphere. There is a reminiscence of the *Ancient Mariner*
in terms of the compulsion and the fatalistic recital, even
down to the technical handling of the dialogue within the
form. There are parallels too with 'Christabel', and in fact
both Coleridge and Chatterton would appear to be influences.
Verses 1 and 2 ask the question; verse 3 describes the
appearance of the enchanted knight; while the rest of the poem
tells the story of a love which appears to be a form of
demoniac possession. The romantic agony is much in
evidence, and the allegorical suggestions perhaps encompass
the ideas of unhappiness in love, the reduction of individuality
by a consuming love, the slavery of love itself – all these are
present and enhance without overloading the antique, simple
narrative form.

The sedge has wither'd This is the line of the refrain, but it is
  echoed elsewhere, and symbolizes the 'withered' knight.
the harvest's done Again the connection between the knight
  and nature is being emphasized.
anguish moist and fever dew The strong suggestion of
  something unnatural or supernatural is present.
withereth The reiteration again of desolation, waste, reduction.
a faery's child i.e. a spirit, and thus supernatural.

fragrant zone i.e. sweet-smelling girdle.

elfin grot picturesque cave.

Hath thee in thrall i.e. you are enslaved, you are no longer a free man.

starved Perished, affected severely by the cold.

To George and Georgiana Keats Wednesday, 21 April 1819

This is Keats's own conception of 'soul-making'. Here Keats asserts that soul-making is brought about by the inter-reaction of the intelligence, the mind and the world in which we live. He then draws an elaborate analogy in which the world is a school, the human heart is the horn book, and the child able to read is the soul, made from the school and the horn book. Thus the variety of life makes for a variety of individuals, of souls with identities. He comes to the conclusion that man's 'altered nature' is his soul. Keats goes full circle, but not without a laugh at his own long-windedness.

cognomen Nickname, manner of designating.

horn Book Paper containing the alphabet, the Lord's prayer, etc mounted on a wooden tablet with a handle and protected by a thin plate of horn.

Zoroastrians An ancient religion still adhered to by the Parsees in India.

Hindoos Keats probably means here believers in Brahmanism, Brahma being the supreme Hindu deity.

Vishnu The second god of the Hindu triad.

Ode to Psyche

Keats has here obviously adapted the legend of the love of Cupid and Psyche: she was originally mortal, but the poet here makes her a goddess and worships her, as at a shrine. Obviously the fact that Fanny Brawne (to whom Keats was later to become engaged) had moved into Wentworth Place, next door at the time of the poem's composition, is very relevant, and may well be responsible for the poem's strongly physical as well as spiritual aura. The form used here has certain derivations from both Dryden and Milton. The sixty-seven lines are divided into four stanzas, the first being a long invocation containing fine word-pictures, both of nature and of the lovers, while the second is a direct invocation to the goddess which the poet would have Psyche become, with a grandiose verbal and visual suggestion of all the rites that should have been hers. The third verse harks back to pagan times, and then by a subtle repetition of the ritual matter of the second, the poet establishes himself as her 'choir'. The fourth verse elaborates this new priesthood, and then the 'fane', the 'sanctuary', are seen to be within the poet's mind, where he will provide 'delight' for Psyche.

Obviously the poem is, on one level, an allegory; using the classical legend as a starting point for what is more a hymn than an ode in praise of Love, of perfection, of the ideal Beauty. The structure is complex after the early pattern of alternate lines rhyming, and there is almost a lyrical close at the end of the first stanza. Keats said that he had taken 'moderate pains' with this ode, that he had written it 'leisurely', and certainly the care shows. The second verse keeps to the pattern of alternate lines rhyming, with vivid double epithets and an evocation of pagan ritual; while the third, with a more complex rhyme scheme, has the fourteen lines of a sonnet filled with the music of worship. The fourth, slightly longer, is complex but fittingly repeats the lyrical close noted in stanza 1.

enforcement Compulsion.
soft-conched The first of a series of liltingly soft double-barrelled epithets. Here it means 'shaped like a shell'.
Psyche The mortal beauty, later goddess, beloved of Cupid.
budded Tyrian Purple.

pinions The last joints of the wings.

eye-dawn ... aurorean Rosy, fresh, from Aurora, goddess of the dawn.

Olympus' faded hierarchy The chief Gods, now forgotten.

Phoebe's sapphire-regioned star The moon.

Vesper Venus as the evening star; hence the epithet 'amorous'.

virgin-choir A reference to Greek and other pagan ritual.

chain-swung censer i.e. in which incense is burned, but note the vividness of the word-picture.

antique vows i.e. those of antiquity, of olden times.

lucent Bright, shining.

So let me be thy choir Notice the subtle variation in the repetition from the preceding verse, almost as if the ritual, the incantation of worship, has started.

fane A temple.

Dryads Wood nymphs.

the wreathed trellis of a working brain A seminal image; one stemming, perhaps, from Keats's earlier study of anatomy.

Ode on Indolence

'*They toil not, neither do they spin*' (Matthew 6, 28)

This is much less intense and much more loosely constructed than the 'Ode to Psyche'. These are ten-lined verses, regular in construction and rhyme scheme, the first verse seeming almost a rehearsal for the 'Ode on a Grecian Urn'; the figures 'on a marble urn' (see letter of Friday, 19 March 1819 to George and Georgiana Keats, p.111: 'Neither Poetry, nor Ambition, nor Love have any alertness of countenance as they pass by me.' The recurrence of these 'shades' occupies verse 2; in verse 3 they appear again, but here there is some fine natural observation to offset the rather tedious 'conceit'. In the fourth, the poet identifies them (Love, Ambition, Poesy); and in the fifth verse there is the retreat into indolence rather than following any of the temptations, while in the sixth the poet takes his leave of them. The writing is for the

most part undistinguished and repetitive, and the idea is somewhat overworked, with the tone occasionally being raised by
a fine and vivid phrase or some sensitive natural description.

Phidian love A reference to the Greek sculptor Phidias who
  perhaps sculpted the frieze of the Parthenon (the Elgin Marbles).
  He died about 432 BC.
hush a masque i.e. quietly disguised.
throstle's lay Bird-song.
demon Poesy i.e. personal compulsion, that which (I am) tied
  to, forced to do.
A pet-lamb in a sentimental farce i.e. used, made a fool of.

To Fanny Keats, Saturday, 1 May 1819

This ebullient letter shows Keats at his lightest, his spright-
liest, his most inventive and warm best. He is writing to his
sister, wishing to see her but pointing out the difficulties of so
doing. He mocks her liking for the clergyman who is to
confirm her, and indicates, by a string of coinages, that he
needs 'parson-sweetening powder' to make him acceptable.
He then gives himself up to everything that pleases his senses
– health, books, claret, for example – but the tone is vivacious
and full of the fun of life, and a whole-hearted enjoyment of it.

Boxes ... pit i.e. reaching an expensive seat in the theatre by
  walking through the cheap standing area to get there.
me rendre chez vous In order to bring myself to you.
Monsr le Curé i.e. the clergyman.
a cock'd hat and powder Dandified, fashionable.
lady-meal The whole sequence is a fine inventory of the uses of
  powder – for example, for wigs – with the innuendo that a parson
  has need of powder to 'sweeten' him. Keats here indulges lightly
  his own anti-clerical bias.
lady kin Little lady, a term of endearment.
ennui Apathy, indifference.
pad nag Easy-paced horse.

odd fishes ... numskuls Eccentrics ... fools or idiots.
dumb bells i.e. short bars with weights used for exercising the muscles.

Ode to a Nightingale

Keats is said to have written this poem (early in the summer of 1819) after hearing a nightingale singing in the garden of Wentworth Place. It is in eight ten-lined stanzas, similar in structure to parts of the 'Ode on Indolence', but with the introduction of a shorter line towards the end of each verse and a complete regularity of form. After the initial response to the bird's song there is a sustained revelation of the senses, the first stanza being a subtle exploration of the mood, the suffering, the numbness occasioned, almost paradoxically, by the effect of listening to the bird's song and 'being too happy in thine happiness'. The second stanza, longing at first for a 'draught of vintage', considers the prospect of drink affording a kind of oblivion with only the nightingale's song for companionship; the third stanza, with the memory of his brother Tom's death strong upon him, shows the poet seeking to escape from the sufferings of life – 'The weariness, the fever, and the fret' in the fourth he returns to the world of the imagination, the world of poetry which makes joining the nightingale, identifying with it, the supreme fulfilment.

Stanza 5 sees that imagination at work, exploring the 'forest dim' with the eye of memory, so that the poet is able to 'guess each sweet', the known and treasured beauties of nature. This delight in nature gives way in Stanza 6 to a movement of the mood, an extension of 'being too happy in thine happiness', for, at the moment of greatest beauty in the nightingale's song, the poet considers the idea of death: 'To cease upon the midnight with no pain'. And this is in direct contrast to the 'weariness, the fever and the fret' of the third stanza. The idea of death, however, leads by natural contemplation to the immortality of the nightingale through its song in stanza 7, with a lyrical sweep of things historical and spiritual, imaginative and ethereal, so that the ecstasy of the verse, in its movement and rhythm, echoes the bird's song.

Stanza 8 marks the return to earth, the descent from the imaginative associations evoked by the song to the reality of living, with the hint that perhaps all has been a dream. Again the allegorical content of the poem has traced the journey through life, love, the imagination, suffering, poetry, death and, superbly, the immortality of beauty, an indelible theme in Keats. This ode, together with those 'On a Grecian Urn' and 'To Autumn', vies for pride of place among Keats's shorter poems; it is insistent with verbal music, the heightened consciousness that can create a work of art. The song of the nightingale is in itself the expression of complete harmony; and the poem is the verbal outpouring of a soul charged with a like joyfulness in beauty.

hemlock A poisonous umbelliferous plant; the poison obtained from this.

Lethe-wards A coinage from Lethe, the river of oblivion.

too happy in thine happiness Note the repetition in the word-play, like the repetitions in the nightingale's song.

deep-delved i.e. deeply dug.

full-throated A fine double-barrelled epithet; compare its effect with 'tongueless nightingale' in 'The Eve of St Agnes', Stanza 23.

Flora The goddess of flowers.

Hippocrene A fountain on Mount Helicon sacred to the Muses, and said to have been caused by Pegasus striking the spot with his hoof.

beaded bubbles Note the alliteration which conveys the cool tang of the drink.

youth grows pale and spectre-thin and dies The obvious, and acknowledged, biographical reference to Tom.

Beauty cannot keep i.e. what is beautiful is subject to change (except the song of the bird, which is heard down the centuries).

Bacchus The God of wine.

pards Archaic for 'leopards'. Shelley's name for Keats was 'Adonais' ('a pard-like spirit').

Queen-Moon Cynthia or Diana.

Fays Attendants.

verdurous glooms Note the rhythmic sweep of the words, which convey the nature of the darkness.

embalmed Descriptive of the effect of darkness, and associated with death.

guess each sweet Somehow the phrase is inadequate, a falling away from the general level of this stanza.

The murmurous haunt Notice how the alliterative effect conveys the buzzing, an effect also found in 'To Autumn'.

Darkling Unusual, somewhat archaic, usage.

alien corn Note the transference of the epithet – it is 'alien', or foreign to Ruth.

Charm'd magic casements Beautifully imaginative in its escapist language.

like a bell/To toll me The ominous note (forgive the word) is struck. 'Never send to know for whom the bell tolls; it tolls for thee', said the 17th-century poet and preacher John Donne, and the implication here is that death will come to the poet, and the end of the song is 'death' to the imagination, a return to 'forlorn' reality.

fancy ... deceiving elf i.e. the 'spright' of the imagination.

anthem Note the echo of 'requiem', music being used to complement the music of the nightingale.

Ode on a Grecian Urn

The form here, with some deliberate variation in line length, is that of the 'Ode to a Nightingale', and again the musical element, the word-pictures, the sensitive descriptions of nature, the invocation, the running alliteration, the imaginative giving of life to what is complete in itself – the life of art – all cohere to provide a like completeness. Thus the first stanza, from the invocation to the questions, is a wonderful word-picture, endowed with life by the tensions of speculation. The second verse examines the 'unheard' pipes, the youth, the lover, the permanence and thus the impossibility of change in the representation, while the third compares this representation of nature, music and love with the realities of life. Stanza 4 examines the other figures on the urn, the priest and the heifer, and this is followed by the imaginative verbal delineation of the little town behind the setting. The final stanza again reiterates the permanence of art, the only beauty which survives, concluding with the assertion that 'Beauty is truth' – an idea central to Keats's own thought, and to his own artistic creations.

unravish'd bride . . . foster-child Note the warmth in these images – of life and love in life as distinct from the love which is a representation, but they cohere as the poem unfolds.

leaf-fringed Descriptive of the reality of the original setting and of the decoration on the urn.

Arcady Arcadia, a particular haunt of Pan, who was, however, believed to be 'everywhere'.

maidens loth i.e. unwilling to yield.

timbrels See note p.48.

Heard melodies are sweet A fine evaluation of the quality of the imagination, which can give to silence its own music.

A burning forehead and a parching tongue Again the stress on the 'sensations' occasioned by extremes of either worry or love. Keats would be familiar with both.

this pious morn Notice how the artistic creation is vividly evoked by the use of the present – the corollary here being that art 'lives' in the present, hence the technical appropriateness of the tense.

brede Embroidery.

tease us out of thought/As doth eternity i.e. stops us thinking, instead we respond with our feelings to the Beauty – the truth we search for is to be found in its existence, and not by speculation.

Ode on Melancholy

Here again is the use of the ten-lined stanza, with virtually the same rhythmic and melodic form as that of 'Ode on a Grecian Urn'. It was written in May or June 1819 – and Robert Gittings's note on the influence of Burton's *Anatomy of Melancholy* is important. For Burton's strong effect on Keats, see Gittings's *The Living Year*. The first verse lists the superstitions and symbols associated with melancholy, the mood of depression, but in the second verse the manifestations of beauty – the rose, the rainbow, the mistress's eyes, for example – are seen as the natural antidotes to oppression. The third verse, however, underlines the transitoriness of all those ecstatic moments – of Beauty, of Joy, of Pleasure, of Delight – for all have melancholy within them. The poet asserts, however, that only those capable of experiencing ecstasy can also experience the extremes of suffering. Thus the commonplace has been elevated by the language and the faith behind it – Keats's own belief that experience and sensation are the centre of living; to reduce this to simple terms, if we want to scale the heights of happiness we must be prepared to endure the depths of despair. 'To Autumn', with one added line per verse, has the same three stanzas, the perfect form for the short ode.

Lethe See note p.63.
Wolf's-bane Aconite, a poisonous plant.
Proserpine The daughter of Ceres (see note p.46). She was carried off to the infernal regions by Pluto.
death-moth Death's-head moth.
bee-mouth i.e. the taking of pleasure, delight, which changes even as we enjoy it.
her might Depression.
cloudy trophies i.e. metaphor for the triumphing of the mood.

Lamia

This was written during May to September 1819, in heroic couplets after the manner of Dryden, with an alexandrine (for instance, line 30) interspersed from time to time, as well as triplets. Again the source is Burton's *Anatomy of Melancholy*: the story itself is quite clear; the first part begins with Hermes searching for a nymph he desires, and while he is resting he hears a voice bemoaning its owner's fate. The voice comes from a snake who, while beautiful in herself, has a woman's mouth and eyes, and wishes to be restored to a full woman's form. She subsequently reveals to Hermes that she has power over the nymph he is seeking, and then shows him the nymph, as in a dream. He in return grants her her woman's form, and flees with the nymph. Lamia, now miraculously transformed, goes to a valley where she waits to accost the youth for whom she craves.

A retrospective sequence tells us that even when she was in the 'serpent prison-house' she had the power to 'will' her spirit anywhere, and this is why she had fixed on the young Corinthian, Lycius, whom she had seen as a fine charioteer. She knows well that he will pass her that evening, waylays him, speaks, and gets him to look back at her. He begs her to stay with him, and Lamia in reply asks him to take her somewhere where she can 'all my many senses pleasure'. She further tells him that she has lived 'retired' in Corinth, that she has seen him pass there, and that she loves him. Lycius, amazed, charmed, enchanted, is taken with her by a spell to Corinth; arrived, they pass 'Apollonius sage' (Lycius's teacher) and Lycius, ashamed, muffles himself against recognition, while Lamia trembles beside him. They reach a palace 'unknown/Sometime to any, but those two alone'.

Part 1
Lycius and Lamia are enthroned upon a couch, but after some time Lycius becomes aware of the noises and activities of the

outside world. At this Lamia begins to sigh in order to attract his attention, and learns that Lycius, proud of her beauty, wishes to display her in Corinth in her 'bridal car'; Lamia begs him to change his mind, but, seeing that he is indulging a perverse streak and becoming tyrannical, she submits, only asking that she may not be seen by Apollonius. She prepares herself 'In pale contented sort of discontent', and afterwards all and sundry enter the 'secret bowers' (the magic palace) which Lamia has got ready for their guests. But the one who was not invited, Apollonius, appears, and there follows an account of the 'reception'.

Gradually many of the guests become drunk, but meanwhile Apollonius has fixed his eyes full on Lamia; she turns cold, a silence settles on everything, and there is a feeling of terror present. Lycius, overwrought by the effect on Lamia, launches a verbal attack on Apollonius and his icy influence, but the philosopher uses the word 'serpent' and, when he repeats it Lamia vanishes with a scream and Lycius dies. This outline carries a heavy allegorical weighting, one that perhaps evaluates sexual love: puts it into perspective; indicates temptation; emotional and sensual slavery; the assertion of rational will. But the success of the poem lies in its brilliant evocation of atmosphere; dazzling word-and-colour pictures; a mastery of the chosen form of the couplet with its variants. The style is mature, assured, just occasionally bathetic. The balance, the antithesis, of the Pope or Dryden couplet is often used, together with some fine natural observation and some indulgence of the senses – both qualities always to be found in Keats.

1 **the faery broods** Note that these first few lines deal with the replacing of pagan mythology by 'fairy' mythology, hence the mention of Oberon, King of the Fairies.

7 **ever-smitten Hermes** Ever susceptible to love. Hermes, as we have seen, is the messenger of the Gods.

15 **Tritons** i.e. human to the waist, and dolphin below.

30 **To find where this sweet nymph** The first of the alexandrines which vary the movement, the flow of the verse, and which are traceable to the influence of Dryden.

40 **ruddy strife** A bathetic description.

42 **dove-footed** A double-barrelled coinage, perhaps ironic here.

46 **cirque-couchant** i.e. coiled in a circle.

47 **gordian** The phrase 'gordian knot' has become a proverbial commonplace. Here it means intricate complicated twistings and turnings.

48 **Vermilion-spotted** Note the vivid colour effects of this passage.

49 **pard** See note p.64.

55 **penanced lady elf** i.e. forced to be as she was.

56 **demon's mistress, or the demon's self** The kind of repetition within the line which achieves an antithetical balance derived from an established practice in Dryden, and later Pope.

58 **Ariadne's tiar** Ariadne's tiara: reference to the constellation into which Ariadne was turned after her marriage to Bacchus.

63 **Proserpine** See note p.46. Note too that she was allowed to return to earth for half the year.

66 **pinions** See note p.60.

67 **like a stooped falcon** A good economical simile, a mark again of maturity of expression.

74 **Apollo** See note p.16.

78 **Phoebean dart** i.e. the sunbeam.

81 **Star of Lethe** Hermes is thus described because he had to conduct the dead souls to Hades.

84 **Thou beauteous wreath** Fine punning suggestion of the serpent and the symbol of death.

92 **the brilliance feminine** Keats makes much use of inverted word order (cf 'Hyperion'); this is a good early example in this poem.

99 **unseen ... unseen** Note the repetition, very much a part of Keats's method.

103 **blear'd Silenus'** Aged satyr with a reputation for drunkenness and lechery.

114 **warm, tremulous, devout, psalterian** Note the range here of the single-word emphasis, with the unusual last word derived from the 'psaltery', an ancient stringed instrument.

115 **Circean** Derived from Circe, the enchantress who kept Ulysses and his men imprisoned.

133 **Caducean charm** i.e. the rod of Mercury.

136–8 **like a moon in wane ... self-folding like a flower** Fine brief similes which enhance both the pathos and the beauty of the situation.

145 **Nor grew they pale** Again the reference is to reality, to fading and death, as in the 'Ode to a Nightingale'.

148 **besprent** Sprinkled.

174 **Cenchreas** On the isthmus of Corinth.

179 **Cleone** A village on the way to Argos.

184 **flaunted with the daffodils** Perhaps an unconscious echo of Wordsworth's celebrated 'And then my heart with pleasure fills/And dances with the daffodils.'

188 **spread a green kirtle** The latter is a gown, and the image is of dancing to music.

191 **sciential** i.e. possessing knowledge (of love).

192 **unperplex** i.e. disentangle, separate.

195 **dispart** Separate, divide.

198 **unshent** Still innocent.

204 **list** Wanted, wished.

207 **Nereids** Daughters of Nereus; nymphs of the Aegean.

208 **Thetis** A sea goddess, and mother of Achilles.

212 **Mulciber's columns** Mulciber is Milton's name for Vulcan.

piazzian line A continuous line of columns.

225 **Egina isle** In the Saronic gulf.

236 **Platonic shades** i.e. the thoughts or ideas of Plato.

248 **Orpheus-like at an Eurydice** Orpheus descended into Hades to win back his wife, and this was granted provided that he did not look at her as he led her to the upper regions. He became anxious, turned, and lost her forever.

261 **Naiad** See note p.20.

265 **Pleiad** i.e. one of the sisters turned into stars by Zeus.

285 **sleights** Tricks, subtleties.

320 **the Adonian feast** That dedicated to Adonis.

328 **let the Mad poets** The beginning of a bathetic few lines, rather like the 'Why were they proud' sequence in *Isabella*.

329 **Peris** Genii, good fairies, an expression from the Persian.

333 **Pyrrha's pebbles** A reference which goes back to Ovid's *Metamorphoses*, though Keats may be thinking of later adaptations of this. After the Flood had destroyed mankind, Deucalion and Pyrrha dropped stones behind them which became men, hence mankind was reborn.

339 **smote ... save** Again the antithetical balance typical of Pope or Dryden is struck.

347 **So in her comprized** i.e. completely filled, absorbed by her presence.

375 **Apollonian sage** Note the inverted word order for emphasis.

382 **Mild as a star in water** A moment of beautiful and natural, and above all graphic, immediacy.

386 **Sounds Aeolian** See note p.44.

394 **flitter-winged** i.e. able to fly anywhere.

Part 2

1 **Love in a hut** The first six lines are repetitive.

12 **Love, jealous grown** From time to time in *Lamia* there is a kind of heavy personification, again perhaps derived from Dryden. Cupid is 'love' here.

24 **a tythe** i.e. one tenth, a small part.

36 **empery** Dominion, rule.

39 **passion's passing bell** An echo of the *Ode to a Nightingale* ('the very word is like a bell') – here the 'death' of passion.

80 **the serpent** The monster Python killed by Apollo at Delphi.

105 **Of deep sleep** i.e. enchanted into sleeping by her magic (to stop him from questioning her).

125 **mimicking a glade** i.e. in imitation of.

136 **missioned** i.e. ordered.

137 **fretted splendour** Delicately wrought work.

151 **gaz'd amain** i.e. vehemently.

160 **daft** Opposed.

172 **into sweet milk the sophist's spleen** Notice how the alliterative 's' sounds convey, by subtle innuendo, the hissing of a serpent, and thus remind one of Lamia's fear of Apollonius.

179 **wool-woofed** i.e. woven.

185 **libbard's** i.e. leopard's.

207 **nectarous cheer** i.e. intoxicating drinks.

224 **willow** i.e. signifying weeping.

226 **thyrsus** The staff of Bacchus.

229 **Do not all charms fly** These few lines contain the theme of the poem – reason as against sensuality and over-indulgence, *and* reason as opposition to the wonder and mystery of life is what is being underlined here. Seen in immediate context, though, the power of reason is given a considered stress, since Lamia is 'erewhile' reduced, and she appears to represent evil or temptation.

275 **deep-recessed** Compare 'green-recessed' in Part I, line 144.

285 **proud-heart sophistries** Arrogant false reasoning.

301 **Keen, cruel, perceant, stinging** Again a splendid variety of single word effects, strongly physical. 'Perceant' means 'piercing'.

King Stephen: a Fragment of a Tragedy

This fragment was written in August 1819, and reflects Keats's love of Shakespeare and his inherent dramatic ability. The King's army is in retreat, and, as he berates his men, one of his supporters arrives, Baldwin, defeated by the Earl of Chester. Stephen declares that he will not accept defeat himself, while in the next scene we are taken, in true Shakespearian manner, to another part of the battlefield, where captains report to Gloucester that Stephen is still fighting, that Baldwin has been captured, and that 'Royal Maud' has invited 'noble Gloster' and his followers to a banquet; a second knight arrives to report the nobility of Stephen's resistance, and Gloucester goes to seek him out. In Scene 3 Stephen, asking for a sword, is approached by De Kaims and other knights; he refuses to surrender, and says that he will only give in to Robert of Gloucester. He is stabbed by a common soldier, and then asks De Kaims to kill him quickly, for he will not be led 'by mean hands .... From this so famous field'. The historical, factual background to this fragment is the battle of Lincoln. Stephen, who had alienated the barons by his extravagance and his use of foreign mercenaries, was defeated by Gloucester in 1141 and taken prisoner.

Scene 1

casing Encasing.

plashy meads Muddy fields.

flurried manes i.e. excited, agitated.

rowel Spiked revolving disc at the end of a spur.

How like a comet Strongly Shakespearian tone about this image.

well-breath'd i.e. recovered.

unaffronted i.e. unbeaten.

a brag A boast.

scutcheon A shield with armorial bearings.

The diadem The crown.

Scene 2

our chroniclers i.e. those who write the history of our deeds.

throng'd towers i.e. crowded (in expectation).

Pallas ... Ilion The reference is to the goddess Pallas Athene, who was on the Greek side in the siege of Troy (Ilium).

His valour still ... The whole passage is strongly reminiscent of the reports of Macbeth's bravery to Duncan.

falchions Broad, curved, convex-edged swords.

morions A helmet without a visor.

Mars The god of war.

Scene 3

Bellona's Another echo of Macbeth, who is referred to as 'Bellona's bridegroom' in Act I, Scene 2 of *Macbeth*. Bellona was the Roman goddess of war.

the labourer Cain Who slew Abel (see Genesis, 4, 8).
Pylos ... Nestor's Nestor was the King of Pylos, and one of the
 Greek leaders in the siege of Troy.
vail Surrender.

(There follows a fourth scene in which Maud hears of
Gloucester's courteous treatment of Stephen in his own house;
already she displays hints of the arrogance for which she
became noted).

To George and Georgiana Keats, Saturday, 18 September 1819

This extract illustrates the nature of Keats's sense of humour,
and also that of his friend Charles Wentworth Dilke. It shows
Brown's own vanity by innuendo, and Dilke's capacity for
mocking it by an embarrassing and direct repeating of what
was said. Again it shows Keats's dramatic sense, for Dilke's
movement from window to window has the elements, the
timing, of farce.

lauding him i.e. praising him extravagantly.

To Autumn

Written in September 1819, this is perhaps the most complete
and unified of Keats's odes. The poem conveys a feeling of
tranquillity, achieved by the use of simple metaphors. The
form is that of the 'Ode to a Nightingale', with an additional
line that conveys the *leisure* of the season; and there is an
absence of shorter lines which tend to stress the movement of
mood in the earlier poem. The alliteration, the associations,
the lushness, the grand and sustained range of the personification – all these combine to give us the finest of short odes.
There is too a dignity about the utterance, with a wealth of
imaginative observation and association that is raised to

sublimity by the close texture of the language, the permanence of seasonal nature, which the countryman sees today – and the reader in his mind's eye for ever.

Season of mists Note the immediate but intimate invocation.

And fill all fruit Note the lushness of the description, so that one feels the ripeness and the weight.

winnowing i.e. separating the chaff from the grain.

swath i.e. of corn.

stubble-plains Fine coinage to stress the stumps of grain sticking up after the harvest.

And gathering swallows twitter Heralding their departure for another summer, a fine way of stressing the cycle of nature and thus the permanent cycle of life epitomized by the contemplation of autumn.

To John Hamilton Reynolds, Tuesday, 21 Sept 1819

A letter which should be read in conjunction with the poem above, for it complements it in so many ways, more particularly in the manner of mood. In this letter Keats praises Chatterton, and also says why he has given up *Hyperion*; he asks Reynolds to mark lines from the poem reflecting 'false beauty proceeding from art', and others as 'the true voice of feeling'. But Keats admits that he cannot do so himself.

Chatterton Keats read much of his verse, and was influenced by some of it. Chatterton (1752–70) died a few months before his eighteenth birthday.

Miltonic inversions i.e. imitations of the word order used by Milton.

The Fall of Hyperion, a Dream

The opening lines are in defence of poetry and the visions or dreams that poetry can engender. Keats imagines himself in a delightful place where he has plenty to eat and drink; in fact he sinks down after a particularly potent 'domineering potion'. When he wakes, he finds that the fair trees and arbour have disappeared, and that he is in an 'old sanctuary'. There he sees 'in a mingled heap confus'd' . . .

> Robes, golden tongs, censer, and chafing dish,
> Girdles, and chains, and holy jewelries –

Then he approaches an altar, tries to ascend the steps, and is stricken by a cold numbness; but once he has touched the first step he finds that he is able to move up. The prophetess tells him that he must go up before it is too late, and at this stage, if not earlier, we become aware of the fact that this is an allegory.

The prophetess of the shrine is Moneta, formerly known as Mnemosyne. The poet's dialogue with Moneta has obviously cost him much inward debate as well, since it covers the seeking of a spiritual 'height', the rejection of selfishness, the working for humanity which in itself is superior to 'dreaming'. The poet feels that he himself may be merely a dreamer, but the high ideal of the poet is before him, and this ideal must not be abused. The 'tall shade' reveals who she is, and that Saturn's image is at the foot of the shrine, and the poet sees her face, and is greatly moved by her eyes, longing to know what is 'Behind enwombed'. He appeals to her, and suddenly finds himself 'Deep in the shady sadness of a vale' – the opening line of 'Hyperion'. The poet's aim now, as he puts it, is to 'see as a God sees', and once more the lines describing the 'fallen Divinity' of Saturn are used as the end, so to speak, of the earlier beginning. The form, as in the previous 'Hyperion', is that of blank verse. Although there are signs of some falling off in power, there are also vivid and sensitive gains in economy of structure and individual quality.

Fanatics have their dreams i.e. religious groups.
bare of laurel i.e. poetry.

Caliphat A reference to the jealous wife of the Caliph in *The Arabian Nights* who used a drug on one of her rivals.

the scarlet conclave i.e..the cardinals who elect the Pope.

Like a Silenus See note p.69.

faulture Keats's own coinage, probably meaning 'feebleness'.

chafing-dish Censer.

holy jewelries All the things described are part of religious ritual.

When in mid-May The beginning of a complex, rather beautiful simile, somewhat in the Miltonic manner.

maian incense From Maia, daughter of Atlas, mother of Hermes, to whom sacrifices were made in the month of May.

utterance sacrilegious Notice the Miltonic inversion.

sooth voice i.e. smooth.

Pythia's spleen Pythia delivered the oracles of Apollo. She, like Moneta, was a woman.

Of all mock lyrists These lines appear to be an attack on false poets – Keats would consider Byron, for example, to be one of them.

About a golden censer Note that this is a repetition, a ritual consciousness which is echoed in the verse.

Moneta Another name for Mnemosyne, but perhaps connected with Minerva, the goddess of wisdom.

lang'rous Languid.

globed brain Keats is probably thinking here of the lobes of the brain.

electral An obvious abbreviated version of 'electrical'.

pin'd Wasted.

act adorant Again the inversion; it means 'prostrating myself'.

The pale Omega i.e. the last representative of the Titans.

Deep in the shady sadness The opening of 'Hyperion'.

His antient mother yet There have been some variants, but we are now in the first Hyperion, and the poem continues from here, with sections from the first Hyperion included until it is abandoned at line 61 of Canto II.

Extract from The Cap and Bells

This is the final poem of Keats's life, belonging to the winter of 1819–20. The verse form is that of 'The Eve of St Agnes'. Certainly there is humour in the first stanza: Keats's friend Brown has said that it was written chiefly for amusement until Keats's health compelled him to break off. The first verse here sets an evening scene, with much play on the gas-lighting introduced into London in 1807. Eban is setting off on an errand when it begins to rain, so he gets into a coach. The rest of the extract is a satirical account of the inadequacy of the London hackney-coaches of the time.

scaith Injury.
Eban A name obviously associated with 'ebony'.
Incognito Anonymous, unidentified.
smelling-bottle ... allies i.e. smelling-salts as protection against the foul smells of the alleys.
hurdy-gurdies Street music from a type of early barrel-organ.
gallies i.e. where criminals were sent to row.
jarvey The driver of the coach.
linsey-wolsey The lining of wool mixture.
glass Window.
litter A pun on the mess in the vehicle and the old-fashioned litter in which people were conveyed.
fiddle-faddle Time-wasting.
lazar-house i.e. the lowest grade of hospital for the poor.
A dull-eyed Argus Argus possessed a hundred eyes, so the implication is that the driver is always on the look-out for any hint of a fare.
tilburies ... phaetons ... Curricles Varieties of light carriage.

To Fanny Keats, Tuesday, 8 February 1820

A fine conversational letter in which Keats shows that his capacity for observation in his sickness – his sharpness and his interest and his imaginative response to the commonplace –

have not declined. In some ways it is a moving letter, a cheerful tone being maintained throughout. At this stage Keats's liveliness has not deserted him.

a Pot boy i.e. One who serves at a public-house.
bobbins Reels of thread.
french emigrant i.e. a refugee from France during the period of its Revolutionary wars, which ended with Napoleon's defeat at Waterloo in 1815.
the tongues and the Bones Keats is punning here, and the remark is doubtless derived from Bottom in *A Midsummer's Night's Dream*, Act iv, Scene 1.

To Fanny Brawne, June 1820

Another moving letter, expressing the fear that if he goes to Italy he will never recover. It is an intensely subjective and possessive letter, as might be expected from the state of Keats's health. He expresses his jealousy, even of his friend Brown, accuses Fanny of flirtations, and recounts the keen and anguished nature of his own suffering on her account. He says how much he desires her – tells her that she does not know what it is to love – asks her not to write if she has done any-thing which 'it would have pained me to have seen'. He only wants '*chaste you; virtuous you*' – and would rather die than have her be anything else than a person of a 'crystal conscience'. Yet despite all the self-pity, we are aware primarily of the genuine anguish which reason cannot drive away, and of the disease which has here broken a warm, impulsive, lively and above all intensely feeling man.

To Charles Brown, Thursday, 30 Nov 1820, Rome

This letter portends the final phase of Keats's illness, and his feeling that he is 'leading a posthumous existence' away from all he knows – an admission of his being moved by the thought of his friends, and of course by love for Fanny Brawne. There is, too, the sad irony of his having just missed Brown, in passing, before he left England. There is a feeling of an irrevocable fate ('There was my star predominant!'); an acknowledgement of his own tremulousness of mind; his fear that poetry and the need to write it is destructive to his health. There is, too, the overwhelming sense of early death through the associations with his dead brother Tom, and the fear that his sister Fanny may share it ('my sister – who walks about my imagination like a ghost').

Severn The painter Joseph Severn (1793–1879); the friend who accompanied Keats to Rome, and helped to nurse him in his final illness.

Revision questions

1 What qualities do you find in the extracts from *Endymion*? Why do you think that Keats was attacked for this poem?

2 Write an appreciation of any *two* sonnets by Keats, bringing out what you consider to be their individual qualities.

3 By close reference to any *two* or *three* letters, indicate Keats's capacity for enjoying life.

4 Compare and contrast in some detail any *two* of Keats's Odes.

5 By close reference to Keats's verse, say in what ways you find him a *visual* poet.

6 Illustrate Keats's ability to create contrasting atmospheres in any of his poems.

7 Examine Keats's ability to adapt myth or legend in any of his poems.

8 In what ways does Keats show his appreciation of the English countryside? You should refer to at least two poems in your answer.

9 What musical qualities do you find in Keats's verse? Illustrate your answer by quotation and reference.

10 Examine in some detail Keats's qualities as a narrative poet.

11 Write an appreciation of Keats's use of a particular stanza form.

12 By a close look at several of the letters, give an idea of Keats's main theories with regard to poetry.

13 'Beauty is Truth.' How far does Keats's poetry exemplify this idea?

14 Examine Keats's use of figurative language in any two of the Odes.

15 By referring to any of the letters, indicate Keats's sense of humour.

16 What qualities in *King Stephen* lead you to believe that Keats might have become a successful dramatist?

17 With reference to a range of poems, indicate Keats's ability to create vivid word-pictures.

18 Compare and contrast the blank verse in each of the poems on 'Hyperion'.

19 'Keats is the master of mood.' Say whether or not you agree with this statement, by referring to a few of Keats's poems.

20 In what ways is Keats successful in conveying 'sensations'?

21 It has been said that Keats's poetry possesses sensuous qualities. By close reference to any two or three poems, say whether you agree or disagree with this statement.

22 Examine Keats's use of either the mystical or the visionary in his verse.

23 In what ways is Keats's poetry a reflection of his own feeling that he was going to die?

24 From your own reading, indicate what autobiographical elements are to be found in Keats's poetry.

25 Defend Keats from the charge that he is no better than a conscious imitator.

26 What do you occasionally find unsatisfactory or bathetic in Keats's verse?

27 What do Keats's letters tell us of his private life?

28 In what ways is Keats a 'love' poet?

29 Why, in your opinion, has Keats's poetry survived changes in literary fashion and criticism? Give reasons for your answer, and refer to some of the poems closely.

30 Write a detailed analysis of any single poem not mentioned in the questions above, and say why it has given you particular pleasure.